Abingdon's

Where the Bible Comes to Life

Older Elementary 3

Jesus Lives!

Also available from Abingdon Press:

Abingdon's BibleZone™
Preschool 3
Teacher's Guide

Abingdon's BibleZone™
Preschool 3
FUNspirational™ Kit

Abingdon's BibleZone™
Younger Elementary 3
Teacher's Guide

Abingdon's BibleZone™
Younger Elementary 3
FUNspirational™ Kit

Abingdon's BibleZone™
Older Elementary 3
FUNspirational™ Kit

Writer/Editor: Judy Newman-St. John
Story Writer: Dr. Michael E. Williams
Production Editor: Vicki Hines
Production Editor: Betsi Hoey Smith
Production and Design Manager:
R. E. Osborne
Designer: Paige Easter
Cover Photo: Sid Dorris
Illustrator: Jim Padgett
Illustrator: Charles Jakubowski
Illustrator: Bob Jones

Abingdon's
Bible ZONE™

Older Elementary 3

Where the Bible Comes to Life

JESUS LIVES!

Abingdon Press
Nashville

Abingdon's
BibleZone™
Where the Bible Comes to Life
Older Elementary 3

Copyright © 1998 Abingdon Press

All rights reserved.

No part of this work, EXCEPT PATTERNS AND PAGES COVERED BY THE FOLLOWING NOTICE, may be reproduced or transmitted in any form or by any means, electronic or mechanical, including photocopying and recording, or by any information storage or retrieval system, except as may be expressly permitted by the 1976 Copyright Act or in writing from the publisher. Requests for permission should be addressed in writing to
Abingdon Press, 201 Eighth Avenue South, Nashville, TN 37203.

ISBN 0-687-09272-8

Unless otherwise noted, Scripture quotations are from the *New Revised Standard Version of the Bible.*
Copyright © 1989 by the Division of Christian Education
of the National Council of Churches of Christ in the USA.
Used by permission. All rights reserved.

Scripture quotations identified as *Good News Bible*
are from the *Good News Bible: The Bible in Today's English Version.*
Old Testament: Copyright © American Bible Society 1976, 1992;
New Testament: Copyright © American Bible Society 1966, 1971, 1976, 1992.
Used by permission.

ANY PATTERN may be reproduced for use in the local church or church school,
provided it is marked as **Reproducible** and the following copyright notice is included:
Permission granted to copy for local church use. © 1998 Abingdon Press.

A Cassette accompanies this resource and can be found in the FUNspirational Kit™ (0-687-093627).
On the Cassette are all masters ℗ Brentwood Music, Inc. and Benson Records, Inc., both divisions
of Provident Music Group, One Maryland Farms, Brentwood, TN 37027. All rights reserved. Used
by permission. Unauthorized duplication prohibited.

Art Credits:
Pages 19, 20, 31, 44, 55, 79, 92, 104, 128, 140, 152, 164: Jim Padgett
Pages 32, 68, 80, 116: Charles Jakubowski
Page 56: Bob Jones
Pages 17, 76, 78, 102, 114: Bob Jones. © 1998 Abingdon Press.
Pages 16, 112: Megan Jeffery. © 1998 Abingdon Press.

98 99 00 01 02 03 04 05 06 07 – 10 9 8 7 6 5 4 3 2 1
MANUFACTURED IN THE UNITED STATES OF AMERICA

Table of Contents

Jesus Lives!

Bible Units in the Zone ... 6
About BibleZone™ ... 7
Welcome to the Zone ... 8
Older Elementary ... 9
The Moneychangers ... 10
The Last Supper ... 22
In the Garden ... 34
Peter's Denial ... 46
To the Crucifixion ... 58
The Resurrection ... 70
Walk to Emmaus ... 82
Jesus and the Fishermen ... 94
Jesus and Levi ... 106
Jesus, Mary, and Martha ... 118
Jesus and Zacchaeus ... 130
The Woman at the Well ... 142
Jesus and Mary ... 154
GameZone ... 166
ArtZone ... 168
Make the Bible the Book They Love ... 170
Enter the Story Zone ... 171
Nametags ... 173
Song: "The Bible Zone" ... 174
Evaluation ... 175

Bible Units in the Zone

1. Holy Week and Easter

Bible Story	Bible Verse
The Moneychangers	Luke 19:46
The Last Supper	Luke 22:19
In the Garden	Mark 14:36
Peter's Denial	Mark 14:71
To the Crucifixion	Mark 15:39*b*
The Resurrection	Matthew 28:6*a*
Walk to Emmaus	Luke 24:35

2. Friends of Jesus

Bible Story	Bible Verse
Jesus and the Fishermen	Matthew 4:19*b*, adapted
Jesus and Levi	Luke 5:27*b*, 28, adapted
Jesus, Mary, and Martha	Psalm 25:4, *Good News Bible*
Jesus and Zacchaeus	Luke 19:10
The Woman at the Well	John 4:14*a*
Jesus and Mary	John 15:12

About BibleZone™

ZoneZillies™:

ZoneZillies™ are game and storytelling props found in the BibleZone™ FUNspirational™ Kit. Some ZoneZillies™ are consumable and will need to be replaced. These are added for the teacher's convenience.

- slide flute
- 12 smiley face balloons
- butterfly beanbag
- 15 hose
- gold coins
- inflatable fish
- 12 sponge balls
- 12 pairs neon shoelaces
- 6 rubber egg balls
- 12 sticky buddies
- 12 fish erasers
- 10-inch flying disk
- net square
- 12 chipboard hearts
- Cassette with music by Brentwood Kids Music

Supplies:

- Bible for each student
- cassette player
- stiff cardboard & pushpins
- construction paper
- paste or glue
- scissors
- clear tape & masking tape
- crayons, markers, pencils
- plastic sandwich bags
- tray & basket
- costume clothing & jewelry
- M&M candies
- empty butter tubs & lids
- tempera paint & brushes
- large pieces of paper
- 5 small bowls & large jar
- stapler, staples
- cotton swabs
- leisure & news magazines
- pancakes & salty crackers
- magazines & newspapers
- white table cloth
- picture of the Last Supper
- candles for worship table
- 8 plastic cups (2 colors)
- small boxes
- glitter
- craft sticks
- several brooms
- small jars & metal spoons
- pencils & small nails
- Easter egg dyes
- lotion
- paper clips & safety pins
- large paper bags
- paper plates
- yarn & embroidery thread
- 2 pairs of tennis shoes
- large, extra-long athletic socks
- large gloves & blindfolds

Older Elementary 3

Welcome to the BibleZone™

Where the Bible Comes to Life

Have fun learning about Holy Week and Easter and the friends of Jesus. Each lesson in this teacher guide is filled with games and activities that will make learning FUNspirational™ for you and your students. With just a few added supplies, everything you need to teach is included in the Abingdon's BibleZone™ FUNspirational™ Kit.

Each lesson has a ZoneIn™ box:

that is repeated over and over again throughout the lesson.
The ZoneIn™ states the Bible message in words your students will connect to their lives.

Use the following tips to help make your trip into the BibleZone™ a FUNspirational™ success!
- Read through each lesson. Read the Bible passages.
- Memorize the Bible verse and the ZoneIn™ statement.
- Choose the activities that fit your unique group of students and your time limitations.
- Read great storytelling tips in the article on pages 171 and 172.
- Practice telling the BibleZone™ story.
- Gather the ZoneZillies™ you will use for the lesson.
- Gather supplies you will use for the lesson.
- Learn the music for the lesson from the BibleZone™ FUNspirational™ Cassette.
- Arrange your room space so there is plenty of room for the students to move and sit on the floor.
- Copy the Reproducible pages for the lesson.
- Copy the HomeZone™ page for students.
- Copy the Nametags (p. 173) and the words to the song "The Bible Zone" (p. 174) for each student.

Older Elementary

Each child in your class is a one-of-a-kind child of God. Each child has his or her own name, background, family situation, and set of experiences. It is important to remember and celebrate the uniqueness of each child. Yet all of these one-of-a kind- children of God have some common needs.

- All children need love.
- All children need a sense of self-worth.
- All children need to feel a sense of accomplishment.
- All children need to have a safe place to be and express their feelings.
- All children need to be surrounded by adults who love them.
- All children need to experience the love of God.

Older Elementary students (ages 9–12 years old) also have some common characteristics.

Their Bodies
- They are experiencing rapid physical and emotional changes.
- Their growing takes a lot of energy, sometimes leaving them lethargic.
- There are great variations of emotional and physical growth among older elementary age students. They are different from one another and different from who they were just a short time age.

Their Minds
- They are concrete thinkers.
- They are practical planners, working toward logical conclusions.
- They like to identify and express attitudes, ideas, and feelings about unfairness and unjust treatment of people.
- They like to laugh and can be silly.
- They are ready for challenging Bible skills and activities.
- They are ready to increase and use vocabulary related to the Christian faith.
- They are capable of understanding people and places unknown to them.

Their Relationships
- They desire to be similar to all their friends but recognize they are not.
- They may have trouble accepting themselves and others at different stages of their personal development.
- They adopt adult language and can appear to be sophisticated.
- They do not want to appear to be vulnerable or innocent.
- They are beginning to identify themselves as individuals separate from their families.

Their Hearts
- They need caring adults who model Christian attitudes and behaviors.
- They need to verbalize experiences and questions about God and faith.
- They need to serve with others in the community and the world.
- They need to feel they have a personal relationship with God.
- They need a sense of belonging to the church and to the larger faith community.

The Moneychangers

Enter the Zone

Bible Verse
It is written, "My house shall be a house of prayer"; but you have made it a den of robbers.
Luke 19:46

Bible Story
Matthew 21:1-17; Mark 11:1-11, 15-19; Luke 19:29-48; John 2:13-25

When Jesus entered Jerusalem riding on a colt, crowds of people cheered and welcomed him enthusiastically. They spread their cloaks on the ground as a gesture of respect and shouted "Hosanna," acknowledging Jesus as the King who comes in the name of the Lord. However, there were others in the crowd, religious leaders, who were not thrilled over Jesus' presence. They were suspicious and fearful of Jesus. The praise and celebration offered to Jesus at the beginning of Holy Week quickly turned into a painful experience of rejection and denial.

In spite of the cheers and celebration, Jesus knew that the people did not really understand who he was. They thought of him as a strong military leader who would save them from their enemies, not as the the Savior who would bring them eternal peace. Jesus was so saddened and frustrated that he wept.

When Jesus entered the Temple, he saw merchants selling animals for sacrifice. He saw moneychangers exchanging coins showing the image of the emperor for coins bearing no image to be used in the Temple. Jesus became angry and drove the merchants and moneychangers from the Temple. Jesus would not tolerate their profit-making from people who had come to the Temple for the sole purpose of worshiping God.

When Jesus challenged the economic practices, he clearly alienated the elders, scribes, and chief priests. Not only that, the leaders probably were jealous and felt threatened. The Scriptures tell us that the people were spellbound by Jesus' teachings. The mistrust, jealousy, and alienation the religious leaders felt only spurred them to a greater determination to rid themselves of Jesus.

Unlike the other Gospels, the Book of John records the cleansing of the Temple (Jn. 2:13-25) before the Triumphal entry (Jn. 12:12-15). John dramatically describes Jesus using a whip made from cords to drive the moneychangers from the Temple.

Jesus wants us to treat others fairly.

Scope the

ZONE	TIME	SUPPLIES	ZILLIES™
Zoom Into the Zone			
Get in the Zone	5 minutes	cassette player; pages 173, 174	Cassette
The Price Is Right	10 minutes	Reproducible 1C, cassette player, masking tape, construction paper, plastic sandwich bag	Cassette, gold coins
BibleZone™			
Zoom Into the Bible	15 minutes	Bible for each student	slide flute
Run for the Money	10 minutes	Reproducible 1D, table	gold coins, slide flute
LifeZone			
Dig Into the Story	10 minutes	Reproducibles 1A and 1B	none
Sing	5 minutes	Reproducible 1E, cassette player	Cassette
Dizzy Disk	10 minutes	none	flying disk
The Hot Spot	10 minutes	chairs, marker, red construction paper, scissors, cassette player	Cassette
Worship	5 minutes	none	none

Zillies™ are found in the **BibleZone™ FUNspirational™ Kit.**

Zoom Into the Zone

Choose one or more activities to catch your children's interest.

Supplies:
cassette player;
pages 173, 174

Zillies:
Cassette

Get in the Zone

Have "The Bible Zone" **(Cassette)** playing as the students enter the room. **Say: Welcome to BibleZone! This is the FUN place where we will get to know the Bible as OUR book! We will sing, hear Bible stories in new ways, play games, and try out neat ways to make great stuff!**

If the students do not know one another, give them nametags to wear **(page 173)**. Give each student a copy of the words for "The Bible Zone" **(page 174)**. Play the song again and invite them to sing with you.

Supplies:
Reproducible 1C,
cassette player,
masking tape,
construction paper, plastic sandwich bags

Zillies:
Cassette,
gold coins

The Price Is Right

Create a circular path by taping down twenty-one different shapes of construction paper. Photocopy three sets of the cards **(Reproducible 1C)**, but keep only one copy of the "Official Money Changer" card for you to wear. Tape the cards randomly onto the paper shapes. Put small, but different, amounts of **gold coins** in plastic sandwich bags (one bag per student). Put up a sign that says "Temple" in the middle of the circle.

Ask the students to choose a paper shape to stand on. **Say: In Bible times people would go to the Temple in Jerusalem to worship. But in order to do that, they had to pay a Temple tax and buy special gifts to honor God. The tax and the gifts could be bought only with Temple coins, so the worshippers had to go to moneychangers to exchange their foreign money for Temple coins; but the moneychangers were not always honest.**

Explain: In this game you are going into the Temple to worship, but first you must exchange your money and purchase gifts and pay tax. I am the moneychanger. I will start and stop music on the Cassette. When I stop the music, you stop. You must first land on a coin exchange for me to give you your bag of coins. When I have stopped the music and you have landed on a gift card or a stack of Temple coins, you may use your bag of coins to purchase the gift or pay the tax. When you have done both, you may go to the Temple (the center of the circle)—if you have enough money.

When the students realize that everyone does not have the right amount of money to make the purchases, talk about how it feels to be cheated and how Jesus would have felt when he saw people being cheated.

BIBLEZONE™

Choose one or more activities to immerse your children in the Bible story.

Zoom Into the Bible

Supplies:
Bible for each student

Zillies:
slide flute

Say: The Temple was a grand place to see. Imagine the beautiful courtyards and the crowds of people from all over the Roman world. Some say that the Temple had so much gold on it that a person could be nearly blinded if he or she looked at it when the sun was shining brightly. The moneychangers had booths set up to exchange Roman money for Temple coins. There were merchants selling doves and lambs to be used for sacrifices. In the midst of this noise and confusion, Jesus entered the Temple. Let's read accounts from the four Gospels to find out what happened.

Divide the students into four teams. (For ideas of ways to create teams, see page 167.) Be sure each student has a Bible. Ask Team One to read Matthew 21:1-17; Team Two to read Mark 11:1-11, 15-19; Team Three to read Luke 19:29-48; and Team Four to read John 2:13-25. Use the **slide flute** to signal when to begin reading. When everyone has had enough time, use the flute again. **Say: Stop reading. Now we will find out which team can tell us the most about what happened when Jesus went into the Temple.**

Run for the Money

Supplies:
Reproducible 1D, table

Zillies:
gold coins, slide flute

Have one set of the question cards (**Reproducible 1D**) photocopied and cut apart. Ask the teams to huddle in the corners of the room. Pile the **gold coins** on a table in the middle of the room.

Say: I will read a question card and play the slide flute. Your team must huddle and talk about the answer. When you have agreed on the answer, pick one person to run for the money. When the runner gets to the table, the runner picks up as much money as he or she can with one hand. If more than one runner reaches the table at the same time, the runner holding the most coins gets to give the answer. The team scores five points for each correct answer. If the answer is incorrect, the other teams automatically earn two points each. Each time the runners return the money to the pile.

Encourage the teams to have a new runner each time. If any incorrect answer is given, move the question card to the end of the questions and repeat the question again when you reach that question card.

ANSWERS:
1. people buying and selling
2. became angry
3. a house of prayer
4. a den of robbers
5. The Book of John tells us that Jesus made a whip from cords and used it to drive the moneychangers from the Temple. All of the Gospels say he overturned the tables.
6. They became angry because the people were so amazed with Jesus. They began to look for a way to kill Jesus.
7. They were spellbound.
8. in the Temple in Jerusalem.

Bible Story

Making Change
by Michael Williams

Let me make this perfectly clear. I was always just a businessman, an honest businessman. I never cheated anybody in my life and have never had a desire to ever cheat anybody. I provided a service for my customers, something they really needed. And I did a good job of it. That's why I was so upset at the time. I never deserved to be treated this way.

Let me get a deep breath and tell you the whole story. You know, I'm not a young man anymore. I should be at home playing with my grandchildren. But, no. I had to keep working because people need to pay the Temple tax, and I helped them do that.

No! I was never a tax collector. I left that to the priests and the publicans. I was a moneychanger. Please don't start with me. Do you think I haven't heard that old joke about moneychangers—a moneychanger is somebody who changes the money from your hand to his. Do you think I just fell off the fig cart? Do you think I was born yesterday? No, I was born day before yesterday. I have heard all the jokes. There is not a joke about moneychangers I haven't heard. So, just be quiet and listen.

Every year it's the same old thing. I've been at it so long I can change money in my sleep. To tell you the truth, the year always will begin for me one month before Passover. That was when we could start exchanging foreign money for the silver coins from Tyre in which the Temple tax had to be paid. People began to pour into Jerusalem from all over the world, speaking their different languages and carrying their leather bags full of foreign coins. There was absolutely no way they could fulfill their religious duty without my help. So I helped them. What would you have done?

Twenty days before Passover our tables were moved from the marketplace into the courtyard where people entered the Temple. There were so many people needing what we had to offer that we had to be right there where the people were. True, the dove sellers give all of us a bad name, but I had no control over what they did. If they charged too much for a dove, what could I do? I was honest in all my dealings.

The Temple tax was one-half shekel per individual. Our fee for exchanging one currency for another was only a very small portion of that, and we didn't keep that for ourselves.

Then one day we heard that a prophet from Galilee named Jesus had ridden into the city on a donkey, and people greeted him as if he was the Messiah. They threw down palm branches and even their coats in front of him. They were shouting, "Hosanna! Blessed is the one who comes in the name of the Lord. Hosanna!"

Then we got word that he was coming toward the Temple. Well, I was glad. I wanted to get a good look at this prophet they called Jesus. He would come to pay the tax, of course, as any good religious leader would do. The crowd was so thick and the noise of many languages spoken all at once was so loud that I hoped I didn't miss him in all of the hubbub.

Reproducible 1A

Well, I couldn't have missed him if I had tried. First, I heard the sound of the crowd outside change. I figured that it was just the way any group of people greet any famous person. Lots of "Ooooh's" and "Ahhhh's" and people saying, "Do you know who you are?" You know people can act silly when they finally meet someone who they have heard so much about that they think they know him. I glanced up from my work but not for long.

The next thing I knew, doves were flying every direction, and the crowd was scattering even faster than the birds. The bird sellers were on their feet shouting something I couldn't understand. My customers were backing away from my table. People were becoming wild-eyed like people who are afraid but don't know what they are supposed to be afraid of.

In a million years I couldn't have predicted the thing that happened next. The prophet, Jesus, walked right up to my table, looked me in the eye, and said in a very calm voice, almost a whisper, "Get up. I don't want to hit you with the table." I stood up and backed away. He waited quietly until I was several steps back. Then with the most peaceful expression I have ever seen on a human face, he picked up one side of the table and sent money, table, and all flying around the room.

Then Jesus raised his hands as if he wanted everyone to get quiet. *Little chance of that*, I thought. The amazing thing was that they did, get quiet, that is. The many languages stopped for a moment and there was quiet. Out of the silence came a voice that sounded as if it carried a hurt too deep for words. Jesus told us, "God said, 'My house shall be called a house of prayer for all the nations, but you have made it a den of robbers.'"

The words struck me like the blows of someone's fist. Thief! Was this Galilean calling me a thief? I had given my life to help other people worship God. At that moment I wished he had hit me with the table rather than with the words he spoke. Or was he even speaking to me at all? Who was this "you" toward whom he had flung the word "thieves"?

It was over almost as quickly as it had started. I didn't even stop to pick up the money scattered across the floor. I was too old for this. That day marked my retirement from moneychanging. Don't think that I considered myself a thief. I could hold my head up. I could say honestly that I never cheated a soul. But the prophet's words still stung. I heard later that rash words and actions had gotten him crucified. I tell you the truth, it doesn't surprise me.

On the other hand, hardly a day passes that I don't think about what he said. He was trying to get us to hear something. But what was it he wanted us to learn? And why did he ask me to move before he threw the tables over?

It was almost as if I was more important than the money. As if I was more important than my job as a moneychanger. Perhaps this prophet, Jesus, thought that changing lives was more important than changing money. Could it be that throwing over the tables was just his very dramatic way of showing us that?

I still do not know for sure, but whether his words were meant for me or not, they hit their mark in my mind and heart. I can tell you this—I still think about him and that day, and I am a different man for it.

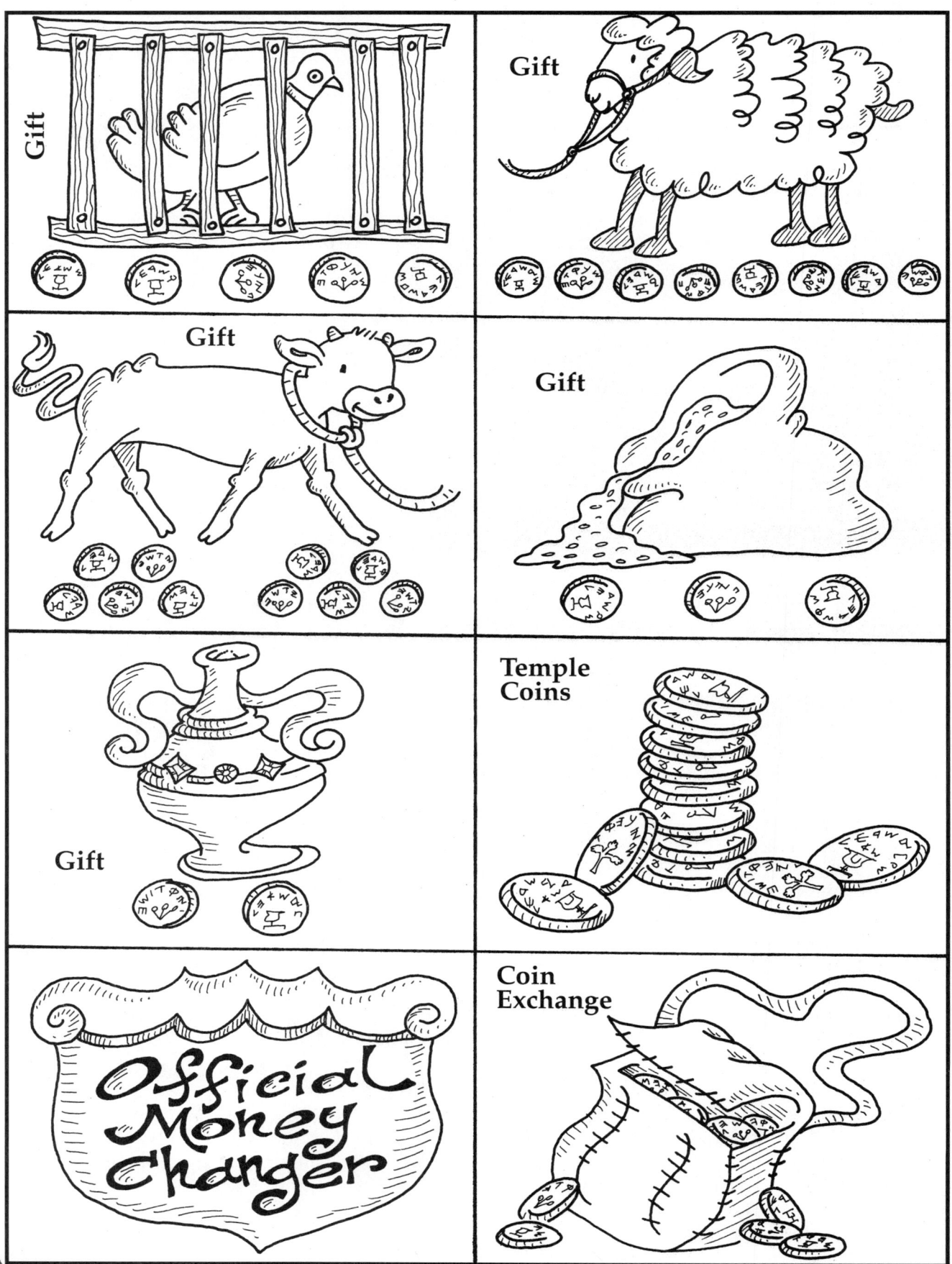

Reproducible 1C

Choose one or more activities to bring the Bible to life.

Dig Into the Story

Ask: Why do you think Jesus turned over the tables and drove the moneychangers out of the Temple? *(Wait for responses.)* **How would you have felt if you had been there and had seen him? What if you were a moneychanger?**

Tell or read the story "Making Change" **(Reproducible 1A and 1B)**. **Ask: How was Jesus changing lives that day? What does that mean for us today?** *(Jesus did not tolerate injustice. He wants us to treat others fairly.)*

Supplies:
Reproducibles 1A and 1B

Zillies:
none

 **Jesus wants us to treat others fairly.**

Sing

Ask: Why should we love Jesus? Why should we praise Jesus? Give each student a copy of the words for the song "Jesus in the Morning" **(Reproducible 1E)**. Play the song on the **Cassette** and ask the students to follow along. Play the song again and invite them to sing. Suggest they help you choreograph the song or they may want to use sign language for the word *Jesus*:

Supplies:
Reproducible 1E, cassette player

Zillies:
Cassette

Dizzy Disk

Ask the students to stand in a large circle. Say the Bible verse three times, each time having the students repeat it with you: **It is written, "My house shall be a house of prayer"; but you have made it a den of robbers.**

Give one student the **flying disk**. Explain: You must say the first word of today's Bible verse; then toss the disk to someone on the other side of the circle. When that person receives the disk, he or she says the next word and tosses the disk. Move quickly and continue until you have said the verse three times!

Supplies:
none

Zillies:
flying disk

OLDER ELEMENTARY 3

Life Zone

Choose one or more activities to bring the Bible to life.

Supplies:
chairs, marker, red construction paper, scissors, cassette player

Zillies:
Cassette

The Hot Spot

Place chairs in a circle. Have one less chair than you have students. In the middle of the circle place a red paper circle on which you have written "The Hot Spot."

Explain: You will walk in a circle around the hot spot while I play music on the Cassette. When I stop the music, everybody grab a chair. The person who does not have a chair has to stand on the hot spot. The person who stands in the circle has to call out something that really makes him or her hot. What is unfair? What have you seen that you believe with all of your heart is wrong? Write down the things the students name.

Say: When you have answered, go back to the circle. I will play the music again and the game will continue.

Continue the game until several students have had a chance to stand on the hot spot.

Supplies:
none

Zillies:
none

Worship

Say: Our lesson today taught us two very important lessons. When Jesus saw the injustice of the moneychangers at the Temple, he would not tolerate it. When we played the game about the hot spot, you named injustices you will not tolerate. Let's think about those injustices and talk about what Jesus would want us to do. Encourage the students to talk about the injustices and to think of rational and positive ways of dealing with them.

Continue: We also learned that Jesus wants us to respect the church. Jesus said that the Temple should be a house of prayer. The same is true for our church. Jesus knew that prayer is an important way in which people grow in their relationship with God.

Ask the students if there are people or situations they would like the class to pray for. Pray together silently. **Close the prayer: Dear God, we thank you for your love. Amen.**

Give each student a copy of HomeZone to enjoy this week.

Home Zone For Students

Prayer Calendar

Make a calendar to help you pray each day of the month. Draw a grid like the one shown on this page. Write the name of the month at the top. Check a calendar to see where the day for that month begins. Begin numbering and add the dates for each day in the month. Write on the squares what you will pray for each day. Add photos or drawings on your calendar. Put your calendar where you will see it everyday to help you remember to pray.

ThinkZone

Read Matthew 21:13, Mark 11:17, and Luke 19:46. Jesus called his house a house of prayer. How would you react if you saw people at church acting in ways you believe are wrong?

Memory Verse

It is written, "My house shall be a house of prayer;" but you have made it a den of robbers.

Luke 19:46

Celebration Pancakes

The day before Ash Wednesday is called Shrove Tuesday or Pancake Day. This name was given because many people confessed their sins and gave up rich foods for Lent. Often they would use up all of the butter, cream, and eggs in the house to prepare for Lent—which often result in pancakes for dinner! You can make your own pancakes. Combine 1 cup flour and 1 teaspoon baking soda. Then add 1 egg and 1 cup of buttermilk that have been mixed together. Warm oil in a hot skillet. Carefully pour small amounts of batter in the oil. When the pancakes have small bubbles in them and look less shiny, carefully use a spatula to turn them over. Cook the second side the same amount of time. Put the pancakes on a plate. Add butter and jelly or pancake syrup and eat!

Jesus wants us to treat others fairly.

Permission granted to photocopy for local church use. © 1998 Abingdon Press.

Older Elementary 3

Question Cards

1. WHAT DID JESUS SEE WHEN HE ENTERED THE TEMPLE?

2. HOW DID JESUS REACT TO WHAT HE SAW?

3. WHAT DID JESUS SAY HIS HOUSE IS?

4. WHAT DID JESUS SAY HIS HOUSE WAS BEING TURNED INTO?

5. WHAT DID JESUS DO TO THE MONEYCHANGERS?

6. HOW DID THE CHIEF PRIESTS AND THE SCRIBES REACT?

7. HOW DOES THE BIBLE DESCRIBE PEOPLE WHO MET JESUS?

8. WHERE DID THE STORY TAKE PLACE?

Reproducible 1D

Song

Jesus in the Morning

Jesus, Jesus
Jesus in the morning
Jesus in the noontime
Jesus, Jesus
Jesus when the sun goes down.

Love him, love him
Love him in the morning
Love him in the noontime
Love him, love him
Love him when the sun goes down.

Serve him, serve him
Serve him in the morning
Serve him in the noontime
Serve him, serve him
Serve him when the sun goes down.
Down, down, down,
Why don't you—

Praise him, praise him
Praise him in the morning
Praise him in the noontime
Praise him, praise him
Praise him when the sun goes down.
Down, down, down.

Arr. © 1996 New Spring Publishing, Inc. (ASCAP), admin. by Brentwood-Benson Music Publishing, Inc.,
All rights reserved. Used by permission.

2 Bible

The Last Supper

Enter the

Bible Verse
"This is my body, which is given for you. Do this in remembrance of me."
                                        Luke 22:19

Bible Story
Matthew 26:17-19, 26-30; Mark 14:12-16, 22-25; Luke 22:7-20

One of the roots of the Lord's Supper is the Passover meal. The Seder, the Passover meal, is observed as a remembrance of God's deliverance of the Israelites from slavery. As Passover is celebrated, God's saving power is claimed for those present at the meal. It is a celebration of the continued saving presence of God with us today as God's people.

The Synoptic Gospels help us understand the connection between our participation in the Lord's Supper and the significance of the Passover meal. On the last night of his life, Jesus joined in the Passover celebration with his disciples. This Last Supper that Jesus shared with his disciples gave the Passover a new meaning. Jesus broke the bread and gave it to his disciples, along with a new understanding of the meaning of bread: "This is my body" (Mark 14:22). He gave thanks over the cup and said, "This is my blood of the covenant, which is poured out for many" (Mark 14:24).

The Hebrew word for covenant meant more than a mere agreement. It meant a bond. In the Bible a covenant between God and humans was always a free promise given by God as an act of grace in return for obedience.

The new covenant is with each of God's people. Jesus wanted his disciples to know that because of his life and death, a new relationship between God and people was possible. When we come to the Communion table, we too are celebrating God's new covenant with us.

At the Last Supper Jesus warned the disciples that he would be betrayed and that he would die. He knew that he must prepare the disciples for the separation they would soon experience. Jesus knew that he must provide strength for them as they faced his death and as they prepared to continue his work without him. When Jesus spoke of his body and blood as symbols of a new covenant, he was helping the disciples to know the importance of his death as a sacrifice for all humankind for the atonement of their sins.

BibleZone™

We remember Jesus and thank God for him.

Scope the Zone

ZONE	TIME	SUPPLIES	ZILLIES™
Zoom Into the Zone			
Get in the Zone	5 minutes	pages 173 and 174, cassette player	Cassette
Passover? Passunder?	10 minutes	none	sponge balls, slide flute
BibleZone™			
Memory Madness	10 minutes	tray, cloth, miscellaneous clothing, jewelry, and accessories	several Zillies from the kit
Zoom Into the Bible	15 minutes	Bible for each student	none
LifeZone			
Dig Into the Story	10 minutes	Reproducibles 2A, 2B, and 2C	none
Swab Art	15 minutes	Reproducible 2D; five colors of paint, five dishes, cotton swabs; or markers	none
Sing	5 minutes	Reproducible 2E, cassette player	Cassette
Please Pax the Cake	10 minutes	four bite-size pancakes per student, white tablecloth, picture of the Last Supper, two candles	none

Zillies™ are found in the **BibleZone™ FUNspirational™ Kit.**

OLDER ELEMENTARY 3

Zoom Into the Zone

Choose one or more activities to catch your children's interest.

Supplies:
pages 173 and 174, cassette player

Zillies:
Cassette

Get in the Zone

Have "The Bible Zone" **(Cassette)** playing as the students arrive. **Say: Welcome to BibleZone!** If you have any new students, take time for introductions and tell them what your class experienced last week. Give out nametags if necessary **(page 173).**

Give each student a copy of "The Bible Zone" **(page 174)** and invite everyone to sing along with the Cassette.

Supplies:
none

Zillies:
sponge balls, slide flute

Passover? Passunder?

Ask the students to stand in a large circle. **Say: I want each of you to turn to your right. You will still be standing in a circle, but you will be facing the back of the person in front of you. When I blow the slide flute, begin passing the sponge balls to the person behind you. If the person in front of you passes the balls "over" (his or her head), you pass them "under" (between your legs) to the next person. If the person in front of you passes the balls "under," you pass them to the next person "over." Keep the balls going around the circle as fast as you can. Let the person know you are passing the sponge balls by saying, "Passover!" or "Passunder!" as you pass them.**

Give a student two **sponge balls.** Blow the **slide flute** as a signal for the game to begin. Walk around the circle and give the student passing the balls two additional balls. Walk again and give another student who is passing or receiving the sponge balls two more. Continue until the students seem to have all the sponge balls they can manage. Encourage the students to pass the balls faster and faster.

Say: Long, long before Jesus was born, the Israelites were in slavery. God saved the people and delivered them from captivity. The angel of death passed over the homes of the Israelites, and their firstborn were spared. The Jewish people had a special holiday every year to celebrate the Passover and to remember how God delivered them from Egypt. The Passover celebration has continued from that time. Jesus celebrated Passover with his disciples in the upper room. He gave new meaning to the meal when he shared the bread and wine. We remember this meal as the Last Supper. When we have Communion, we remember the Last Supper and thank God for Jesus.

Choose one or more activities to immerse your children in the Bible story.

Memory Madness

Ask a student to join you outside your classroom. Have different clothes or accessories available for your student to wear: for example, a sweater, costume jewelry, a tie, a hat, a shoulder bag, a backpack, a scarf, and so forth. Prepare a tray that has several of the **Zillies** on it. Cover the tray with a cloth so that the Zillies cannot be seen.

Go back into the classroom. Ask everyone to stand in a semicircle. **Explain: We are going to discover just how good our memories are. *(Student's name)* will be carrying a tray in the room. When *(name)* uncovers the tray, look closely to see what items are on the tray.**

Have the student come in the room. Ask him or her to uncover the tray and carry the tray around the semicircle, holding it so that each student has an opportunity to see what is on the tray. Then ask the student to cover the tray and to leave the room.

The students will be expecting you to ask what was on the tray. **Instead, ask: What was *(student's name)* wearing that he or she was not wearing when class first began?**

Talk about remembering. **Ask: What kinds of things are easy to remember? What makes something easy to remember?**

Supplies:
tray, cloth, miscellaneous clothing, jewelry, and accessories

Zillies:
several Zillies from the kit

Zoom Into the Bible

Divide the students into three teams. Ask Team One to read Matthew 26:17-19, 26-30. Ask Team Two to read Mark 14:12-16, 22-25. Ask Team Three to read Luke 22:7-20.

Ask the teams to share what they have read in the Scriptures. **Ask: What did Jesus give us to remember?** *(a new covenant)* **How did Jesus give us the new covenant to remember?** *(He said that the bread and the cup should be symbols of his body and blood.)*

Supplies:
Bible for each student

Zillies:
none

 **We remember Jesus and thank God for him.**

Bible Story

The Last Supper
by Michael Williams

Sally had been to Rebekkah's house many times before. After all, they were best friends. Their parents knew each other because Sally's mom, Elizabeth, was a pastor and Becky's mom, Sarah, was a rabbi. They saw each other at meetings and at the yearly Thanksgiving Community Worship Service. In fact Sally and Rebekkah became friends because their moms were friends first.

This evening Sally and her mother were invited to a Seder [sa' der] meal, which was part of the celebration of a holiday called Passover. Sally had never been to this kind of dinner before and was very excited, though it seemed that her mother was almost as excited as Sally. "This is a meal like the one Jesus had with his disciples that we Christians call the Last Supper," her mom had told her. *To take part in a meal like one Jesus had eaten with his friends would be great, and to be able to eat it with your best friend was even greater,* Sally thought.

Becky met Sally and Elizabeth at the door and invited them into the house. Sarah was placing the last of the dishes on the dining room table. After they had all been seated, Sarah began, "What a treat it is to have friends with us to share in our Seder this evening. The Seder meal is a time that we remember a story, and eating is included as part of telling it. In fact the story our meal tonight remembers is called the Haggadah [ha' ga da'], which means telling, since it tells a story of the Jewish people long ago. But it is not just something that happened long ago for us; it happens again every time we tell the story."

Becky's mom said a prayer in Hebrew over one of the cups of wine in front of her on the table, then said in English, "Blessed are you, our God, creator of the universe who has given us the fruit of the vine." She pointed out that there were five cups of wine on the table. The four cups would be used as part of the meal. The fifth cup was for Elijah. That's right, that Elijah from the Bible. It seems that since Elijah never died but went straight to God without passing through death, he might show up at any moment. Sarah explained that in olden days at some point in the meal someone would get up and open the door to the house. Some say that was in case Elijah showed up. Others say it was to show their Christian neighbors that they were not up to any harm behind their closed doors.

Sarah went on to say other prayers, then paused to tell us about the foods that were on the table. There were flat pieces of bread that looked like really big crackers which she called Matzah [mat za]. Sarah explained that the slaves were told by God to leave Egypt in such a hurry that they could not even take time for their bread to rise, so on Passover we eat unleavened bread only. She went on to explain that the Hebrew name for Egypt was Mizraim [miz ray' im], which means the narrows or the tight place.

Reproducible 2A

Permission granted to photocopy for local church use. © 1998 Abingdon Press.

BibleZone™

Whenever we find ourselves in a tight spot, we can remember the slaves in Mizraim, she told us, and how God freed them.

Also on the table there was a mixture of apples, nuts, and spices that Sarah called charoset [huh roh' set] which was to remind us of the clay that the Hebrew slaves used to make bricks. Near that was a strong-smelling dish named maror [ma' ror]. Becky's mother said that this was horseradish and was the bitter herbs that were to be eaten at the Seder to remind us of the bitterness that the Hebrew slaves suffered at the hands of their Egyptian masters. Then there was the shankbone of a lamb and a boiled egg to remind us of the worship that took place at the Temple in Jerusalem in ancient times. Finally, there was some parsley that Sally had seen on plates of food just to make then look more appealing. No one ever ate it. Becky's mom explained that these would be dipped in salty water, then eaten. The salty water, which was in a little bowl at each place where they sat, was to make them think of the tears the slaves cried.

As they began the meal Sarah told Sally and Elizabeth that the telling of the story came in response to questions asked by four children. These questions were about why the family did certain things at the Seder that were different from other meals. She said that all the questions came down to one, "Why is this night different from all other nights?"

Sarah told Sally that since she was the guest this evening, she could ask the question. So she did. "Why is this night different from all other nights?" Sally asked.

Sarah replied, "I'm glad you asked me that," and laughed.

Then Becky's mom went on to tell the story of the slavery in Egypt and how God had heard the people when they cried out for help and had brought them out of the land of slavery and into freedom. At one point she had everyone at the table repeat the names of the plagues that the Egyptians went through: blood, frogs, lice, poisonous beasts, plague, boils, hail, locusts, darkness, and death of the first born.

Each time they mentioned one of the plagues the Egyptians suffered, Sarah told them to pour a few drops of wine from a cup. "Our joy is never complete as long as someone else, anyone else, suffers, even the Egyptians."

Then they went through what appeared to be a long poem in which each line began with the words, "If only you had (done this or that) and not (something else), it would have been enough." Then they sang a song that repeated the Hebrew word *Daiyenu*, which means "It would have been enough."

They ate and they sang and they prayed until the meal was eaten. Becky's mom finished the meal by saying, "Next year in Jerusalem."

Parts of the meal were great, especially the charoset. Parts of the meal were yucky, like the maror. The horseradish burned your mouth and your nose, but Sally guessed that was the idea. Being a slave must have been even worse than eating bitter herbs.

Bible Zone Story

On the way home Sally and her mother talked about the meal they had just shared with their friends. "Can you think of a meal during which we tell a story?" Elizabeth asked.

At first Sally blurted out, "Grandpa always tells stories when we get together for Thanksgiving and Christmas."

"That's true," her mom answered, "but I was thinking of something else."

A story? A story? Sally thought and thought. Just as they turned the corner onto their street, Sally thought of the story. "Communion," she said. "When you serve Communion at church, you tell the story of Jesus and his disciples."

"Yes, just like Becky's mom told the story of the Hebrew slaves just as if it was happening to us today," Sally's mom said. "I tell Jesus' story just like it was happening to us today. Remember I say, 'On the night in which he gave himself for us'? Remember I said that the last supper Jesus shared with his friends was very much like the meals we shared with our friends tonight?"

Sally nodded her head yes. She did remember. Sally had to admit, that was pretty cool.

Reproducible 2C
Permission granted to photocopy for local church use. © 1998 Abingdon Press.

Life ZONE

Choose one or more activities to bring the Bible to life.

Dig Into the Story

Say: The Passover celebrates the memory of God delivering the people of Israel from slavery in Egypt. During the meal the people remember that God sent several plagues to persuade Pharaoh to free the Israelites. The last plague was the death angel, sent to kill the first born child in every household, except those marked with the blood of a newly slain lamb. The death angel "passed over" the houses that were marked. The celebration of Passover involves joy and thanksgiving for God's saving action in history. Such thoughts were with Jesus and the disciples as they sat down to the meal in the upper room. Let's hear a story that helps us to understand more about Passover and why it is important to us as Christians.

Tell or read "The Last Supper" **(Reproducibles 2A, 2B, and 2C)**.

Supplies:
Reproducibles 2A, 2B, and 2C

Zillies:
none

> **ZONE IN:** We remember Jesus and thank God for him.

Swab Art

Give each student a copy of the art of the bread and cup **(Reproducible 2D)**. Ask the students to read today's Bible verse with you as it is written on the art: "This is my body, which is given for you. Do this in remembrance of me" (Luke 22:19).

Say: When we share the Lord's Supper or Holy Communion, we remember what Jesus said. He used the bread and the cup to help us remember his body and blood and the sacrifice he would make for us. Through Jesus we have a new relationship with God.

Place five small dishes of paint and cotton swabs in the middle of the work area. Ask the students to use each cotton swab for only one color of paint and not to mix the colors. Suggest they put color on each letter of the Bible verse. Or place markers of bright colors where the students can share them. Encourage them to take their posters home to put in their rooms.

Supplies:
Reproducible 2D, five colors of paint, five dishes, cotton swabs; or markers

Zillies:
none

OLDER ELEMENTARY 3

Life

Choose one or more activities to bring the Bible to life.

Supplies:
Reproducible 2E, cassette player

Zillies:
Cassette

Sing

Give each student a copy of the words to the song "I've Been Redeemed" **(Reproducible 2E)**. Play the song on the **Cassette** and ask the students to follow along. Play the song again and invite them to sing with you.

Supplies:
four bite-size pancakes per student, white tablecloth, picture of the Last Supper, two candles

Zillies:
none

Please Pax the Cake

Before class prepare four bite-size pancakes for each student. Prepare a worship table using a white tablecloth, two candles, the pax cakes (bite-size pancakes) on a plate, and a picture of the Last Supper.

Ask the students to sit in the chairs around the table. **Say: We have been talking about the Last Supper. No matter how we have lived during the last week, God accepts us and forgives us when we ask for forgiveness. As we share the meal, we celebrate the new covenant in Jesus Christ. Our worship today will be a pax cake service. This service was first used almost a thousand years ago in England. Pax is a Latin word that means peace. People who had argued during the past year met and ate pax cakes as a way of asking for and receiving forgiveness.**

Pass around the plate and ask the students to take four cakes each. Tell them you will let them know when to eat them. Ask them not to talk during the service. **Say: Eat the first cake. As you eat, think of the members in your family you have argued with this year. Forget and forgive these quarrels. They have been forgiven.** (Pause while the students eat.) **Eat the second cake. As you eat, think of the friends you have argued with this year. Forget and forgive these quarrels. They have been forgiven.** (Pause while the students eat.) **Eat the third cake. As you eat, think of pets, animals, or birds that you have been unkind to or thoughtless of this year. Forget and forgive these treatments. They have been forgiven.** (Pause while the students eat.) **Eat the fourth cake. As you eat, think about other persons you have argued with this year—people you know and people you do not know. Forget and forgive these arguments. They have been forgiven.** (Pause while the students eat.) **Pray: Thank you, God, for your forgiveness. We know that your gift of forgiveness is possible because of Jesus. Amen.**

Give each student a copy of HomeZone to enjoy this week.

Home Zone For Students

Remember When?

Think of a time you spent with someone who is really special to you. You can create a unique card to send to that person to remind him or her of your special time together.

Find things that remind you of that time; for example, photos, ticket stubs, an advertisement. If you want to use flowers or leaves, press them between two sheets of paper inside a big, thick book to flatten them.

Fold a sheet of colored paper in half to create a card. Write a note on the inside of the card about your special time. Put a little glue on each item and press it onto the front of the card. Let the card dry. Cover the front of the card with clear self-adhesive paper by starting at one end and rubbing your fingers over the paper as you lower it. Trim the extra self-adhesive paper from the edges of the card.

ThinkZone

Have you heard the expression "You are what you eat"? If that is true, what does eating the bread and drinking the juice during Communion mean to you?

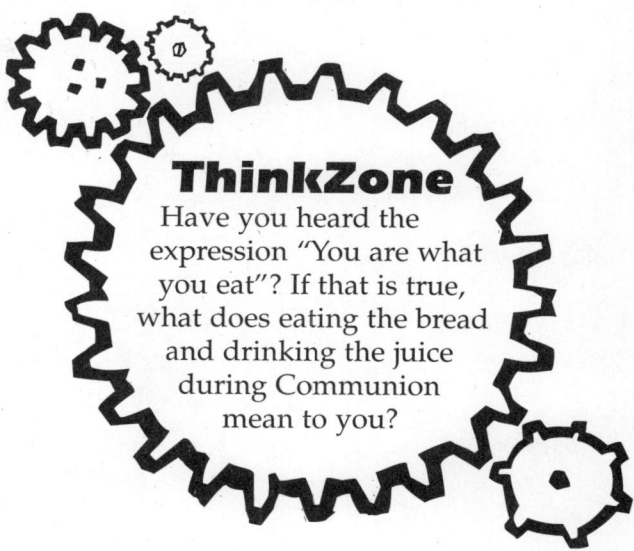

Remember Rolls

Bake delicious rolls to help your family remember special occasions. Pick a meal when your family will all be together and serve the rolls. As each person takes a roll, ask him or her to tell about a special family occasion he or she remembers.

You will need:
- one 8-ounce can of refrigerated crescent dinner rolls
- ground cinnamon
- ½ cup mini chocolate chips
- confectioner's sugar

Heat an oven to 375 degrees. On an ungreased cookie sheet unroll the dough to make eight triangles. Sprinkle a little ground cinnamon on each triangle. Spread one tablespoon of mini chocolate chips on each triangle and press them into the dough just a little. Start at the shortest side of the triangle and roll the dough to the opposite point. Bake 10 to 12 minutes or until golden brown. Sprinkle confectioner's sugar over the top of each roll. Serve them while they are warm.

Memory Verse

"This is my body, which is given for you. Do this in remembrance of me."
Luke 22:19

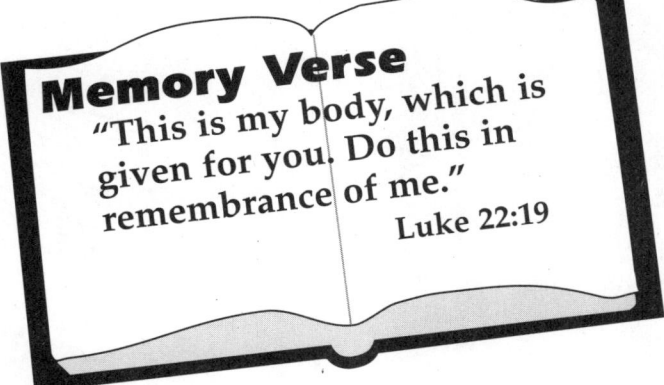

We remember Jesus and thank God for him.

Permission granted to photocopy for local church use. © 1998 Abingdon Press.

Older Elementary 3

Song Zone

I've Been Redeemed

I've been redeemed by the blood of the Lamb,
I've been redeemed by the blood of the Lamb,
I've been redeemed by the blood of the Lamb.
I'm going to the promised land;
All my sins are washed away.
I've been redeemed.

God sent His son to die for me,
God sent His son to die for me,
God sent His son to die for me.
So I could live eternally;
All my sins are washed away.
I've been redeemed.

You can talk about me just all you please,
You can talk about me just all you please,
You can talk about me just all you please.
I'll talk about you when I'm on my knees.
All my sins are washed away
Cause I've been redeemed.

I'm on my way to Heaven above.
See, I'm on my way to Heaven above.
I'm on my way to Heaven above,
I'm filled with God's fantastic love,
All my sins are washed away cause
I've been redeemed.

Arr. © 1996 New Spring Publishing, Inc. (ASCAP), admin. by Brentwood-Benson Music Publishing, Inc., All rights reserved. Used by permission.

3 BibleZone

In the Garden

Enter the Zone

Bible Verse
He (Jesus) said, "Abba, Father, for you all things are possible; remove this cup from me; yet, not what I want, but what you want."
                                                            Mark 14:36

Bible Story
Matthew 26:36-50; Mark 14:32-46; Luke 22:39-47, 54

The Gospel of Luke tells us that Jesus often went to the Mount of Olives to pray. Just a short walk from the eastern walls of Jerusalem, the Mount of Olives provided Jesus solitude as he prayed to God.

Jesus had asked the disciples to go with him to the Mount and had warned them to "pray that you may not come into the time of trial" (Luke 22:40b). The trial Jesus spoke of may have been the temptation of the disciples to forsake their commitment to Jesus in the days that were to come.

The disciples must have sensed that something important was happening. Nevertheless, their human weakness appeared, and they were unable to stay awake during this important time for Jesus. They may have been emotionally exhausted by the recent events and the forthcoming loss of Jesus.

Luke 22:42 symbolizes the "cup" as that which is given by God. Earlier in the evening Jesus had shared the cup of blessing with his disciples. In his prayer Jesus asked that the cup be removed from him; then he fully surrendered to God's will. Even though God called Jesus to drink from the cup, God strengthened Jesus to do God's will and to accept the suffering he would have to endure.

Help your students realize that in his agony Jesus turned to God for help. Help your students learn to pray by making prayer a natural part of class time. Prayer does not have to be reserved for the end of class or for a separate worship experience. When you feel especially thankful for something that has happened in your classroom, ask your students to pause for prayer. Look for times for the boys and girls to express their feelings to God through prayer.

God always hears our prayers.

Scope the Zone

ZONE	TIME	SUPPLIES	ZILLIES™
Zoom Into the Zone			
Get in the Zone	5 minutes	page 173, cassette player	Cassette
Great Cup Challenge	15 minutes	eight plastic cups (four of each color); masking tape	slide flute, shoelaces
BibleZone™			
Zoom Into the Bible	15 minutes	Bible for each student, large piece of paper, markers, Reproducible 3C	none
Alley What?	10 minutes	Reproducibles 3A, 3B, and 3C	none
LifeZone			
Prayer Tag	5 minutes	Reproducible 3D, cassette player, tape	Cassette
Fill It Up	10 minutes	large cup, pens, slips of paper	none
SIng	5 minutes	Reproducible 3E, cassette player	Cassette
Easy As Pie	10 minutes	chalkboard and chalk OR large piece of paper and marker	flying disk
Worship	5 minutes	cup with prayers in it	none

Zillies™ are found in the **BibleZone™ FUNspirational™ Kit.**

OLDER ELEMENTARY 3

Zoom Into the Zone

Choose one or more activities to catch your children's interest.

Supplies:
page 173, cassette player

Zillies:
Cassette

Get in the Zone

Welcome each student enthusiastically. Have "The Bible Zone" on the **Cassette** playing as they enter the room. If you have any new students, take time for introductions and tell them what your class has been experiencing. Give out nametags if necessary **(page 173)**.

Supplies:
eight plastic cups (four of each color); masking tape

Zillies:
slide flute, shoelaces

Great Cup Challenge

Use masking tape to create two parallel lines down the middle of the room. Leave two feet of space between the lines. Assign one color of cups to each team. Place four cups of one color on the outside of each parallel line, placing all cups equal distances from one another (see sample layout below). **Say: We will call the area inside the lines "The Garden."**

Divide the class into two teams (team a and team b). Then ask the members of each team to pick partners. Give each pair of partners a **shoelace**. Ask the partners to stand side by side. Tie a shoelace around one leg of each person so that the partners are tied together.

Have the sets of partners for each team to stand on opposite sides of the tape outside "The Garden." Have the pairs stand with some space between them.

```
      a  a                a  a
_____

              The Garden
_____
      b  b                b  b
```

Say: I will use the slide flute to signal when to begin and when to stop. Partners, you must work together to kick the cups out of "The Garden" and onto the side of the other team. You will have to work fast to keep the cups from being passed to your side. When I use the slide flute, I will count how many cups are on each team's side. After all the partners have played, I will do a grand total to see who wins the great cup challenge. The team with the fewest cups on its side wins.

Repeat play until all the teams have played. Keep the score. **Say: Today we will learn about a time that Jesus went to the garden and a very important cup that he prayed about.**

BIBLEZONE™

Bible

Choose one or more activities to immerse your children in the Bible story.

Zoom Into the Bible

Be certain each student has a Bible. **Say: Our Bible story today is found in three of the Gospels—Matthew, Mark, and Luke.**

Divide the students into three teams. Have Team One read Matthew 26:36-50. Have Team Two read Mark 14:32-46. Have Team Three read Luke 22:39-47, 54. Suggest that the teams divide the verses among themselves.

Prepare a large piece of paper that has three columns. Write Matthew, Mark, and Luke at the top of the columns. Ask one student to be the recorder and to write the answers to the following questions. *(See Reproducible 3C for answers.)*

1. Where did Jesus go?
2. Who went with Jesus?
3. Why did Jesus go there?
4. What did Jesus ask them to do?
5. What did they do?
6. What did Jesus pray?
7. What happened as Jesus prayed?
8. What was used as a sign to betray Jesus?
9. What happened to Jesus then?

Ask the students to help you retell the story from the Bible.

Supplies:
Bible for each student, large piece of paper, markers, Reproducible 3C

Zillies:
none

Alley What?

Read or tell the story "The Prisoner" **(Reproducibles 3A, 3B, and 3C).** (For great storytelling tips, read the article on pages 171 and 172.) **Say: This is an allegory, a story that has characters or events that have a deeper meaning than first appears and are similar to another story.**

Ask: What things did you recognize that are similar to the actual Bible story? Why did one character call himself the ambassador? Why was he going to free the ambassador? What did he mean by "the crime you committed"? How is the prisoner like the disciples? Are you prisoners of anything? *(fear, shame)* **What do you think the newly released prisoner did next? Why?**

Supplies:
Reproducibles 3A, 3B, and 3C

Zillies:
none

Bible Zone Story

The Prisoner
by Michael Williams

Have you ever said you would do something, but you just couldn't do it? I've done that lots of times, too many to remember. Sometimes I would make a promise and ten minutes later I had forgotten I had made it. To tell you the truth, I was not a very nice guy to be around. That is probably why I wound up in trouble so much.

That's why I wound up in this country at the end of the world in this deserted prison. When I was first arrested, I asked them, "What's the charge?"

"What's it to you?" was all they said.

"You can't arrest me unless you charge me with something. I know my rights."

"In this place you have no rights," they said. "We can arrest you because we don't like your looks. We can arrest you and then come up with the reason." They were so smug.

"I want to see my ambassador," I demanded. I wasn't going to take this lying down.

"Oh, I am so sorry. Your country has no diplomatic relations with this country. You have no ambassador." I thought they would laugh next.

With that they threw me into a cell and slammed the door shut. It hasn't been open since. They slide the food, if you can call it that, through a slot in the door just above the floor.

I haven't even seen anybody else. Any other prisoners, I mean. As far as I know, I am the only one here, except for the guards. I never see any other prisoners. I never hear any other prisoners. I never leave this cage. I am like an animal trapped in the wild and sent to a zoo. I just happened to be in the wrong place at the wrong time. I still don't know what they charged me with.

I thought I would live out the rest of my days in this rotten place. Then yesterday evening I heard a lot of noise outside my cell. The guards came bringing with them another prisoner.

"Got some company for you. We didn't want you to get lonesome."

"Thanks, guys." It sounded strange to hear my own voice. I hadn't spoken in so long, I'm surprised I could talk at all.

The new prisoner didn't look like much. He had long hair and a beard, but then so did I from being in this cell for so long. I just didn't have a mirror to see myself. With the new guy I didn't need one. Looking at him was probably a lot like looking at me. The guards threw him on the floor and left.

I walked over to him to see if he was alive and could talk. As I got down to look into his face, he opened his eyes. He stared directly into my eyes, holding me there with his look. Then he whispered, "I'm the ambassador, and I've come to get you out."

Reproducible 3A

Permission granted to photocopy for local church use. © 1998 Abingdon Press.

Then his head dropped, and his eyes closed. He slept for a long time.

Just as I was about to drift off to sleep, he woke up. He sat up slowly and looked around the dark cell. He didn't say a word for a long time. Finally, I asked him, "Do you need anything?" I realized as soon as the words were out of my mouth how dumb that must have sounded. Even if he did need something, where was I going to get it for him? So I added, "Can I help you?"

I thought I heard a faint, "No." I couldn't be sure. Then just as I was about to stretch out for a snooze, I heard his voice again.

"Yes," the voice said, "there is something you can do for me."

"Okay," I said, "What's that?"

"You can stay awake long enough for me to pray. You could keep me company." His voice sounded pretty weak, so I didn't think that would be too hard.

"Okay, just don't expect me to do any of the praying. I'm not the religious type." I wasn't saying anything against his praying. I just didn't want him to expect me to join in.

Well, he started to pray. At least I guess that's what he was doing. It sounded like he was praying in some language I couldn't understand. He just kept going on and on. The only words I could make out were, "bitter cup," and he seemed to keep repeating them over and over.

To tell you the truth, I really wanted to stay awake. This was not one of those promises that I instantly forgot about. I tried as hard as I could to keep my eyes open, but I just couldn't. In spite of everything they just kept drifting closed. I could hear his prayer in the background going on and on.

Suddenly, somebody was waking me up. It was the other prisoner. We were outside in a beautiful spot, not in that cell anymore. But the new guy was upset. He said to me, "Couldn't you wait for me just one hour while I prayed?" Then he walked away.

Well, he went back to praying, and I went back to sleep. The next thing I knew he was waking me up again. We were still outside on this beautiful hillside, and he's asking me again why couldn't I stay awake. I don't know why I couldn't stay awake. So I went back to sleep.

The third time I woke up we were back in the cell. Morning light was beginning to peek through the cell window. The new prisoner was still praying. Then I realize what had pulled me up out of sleep. The guards were beginning to lift the new prisoner up on his knees and take him out of the cell.

As he left I said, "Sorry I couldn't stay awake."

He looked directly at me again and replied, "It's okay. You didn't know what you were doing. See you later."

"No, you won't," one of the guards grumbled.

A little later I heard the footsteps of the guard who always brought me my breakfast. This time, though, he had two trays and something that looked like clothes draped over his arm. He unlocked the door to the cell and set the trays down.

Bible Story

"Here are your clothes," the guard said, "and he said you could have his meal. He wasn't going to need it."

"What happened to him?" I was almost afraid to ask.

"He was executed."

"What for?"

"The crime you were arrested for. So when you finish your meal and get dressed, you're free to go."

As the guard turned to leave the cell, he said back over his shoulder, "He said to tell you he'd see you later, but for the life of me I can't figure out why."

	Matthew	Mark	Luke
1.	Gethsemane	Gethsemane	Mount of Olives
2.	Peter and two sons of Zebedee	Peter, James, and John	Disciples
3.	To pray	To pray	To pray
4.	To stay awake	To stay awake	Not come into the time of trial
5.	Fell asleep	Fell asleep	Fell asleep
6.	To have the cup removed but he would follow God's will	To have the cup removed but he would follow God's will	To have the cup removed but he would follow God's will
7.	No record	No record	His sweat was like drops of blood.
8.	A kiss	A kiss	A kiss
9.	He was arrested.	He was arrested.	He was arrested and taken to the high priest.

Reproducible 3C
Permission granted to photocopy for local church use. © 1998 Abingdon Press.

Choose one or more activities to bring the Bible to life.

Prayer Tag

Make copies of the praying hands **(Reproducible 3D)**. You will need one fewer copies than the number of students in your class. Tape the praying hands on the floor as far apart as possible. Select a person to be "It."

Explain: When the music begins playing on the Cassette, everybody run. "It" will try to get close to you. When I stop the music, find the nearest praying hands and kneel on them. "It" can tag you only if you are not kneeling on the praying hands after the music stops. The person who is tagged becomes "It."

Each time you stop the music, remove a copy of the praying hands from the game. Soon you will have several students who could be tagged and become "It."

Say: In this game we kneeled on the praying hands so we did not become "It." In real life we often kneel to pray. Why do you think we kneel? Why do we pray? What do we pray about?

Supplies:
Reproducible 3D, cassette player, tape

Zillies:
Cassette

Fill It Up

Place a large cup on the table. **Say: We have named several things we pray about. We can take all of those things to God in prayer. Jesus asked that God take the cup from him. We ask that too, when we pray. We ask God to take our concerns and care for them.**

Give each student a slip of paper and a pen. **Say: Think of one concern that you want to give to God. Write that concern on the paper. Then fold the paper and place it in the cup.**

Supplies:
large cup, pens, slips of paper

Zillies:
none

Sing

Give each student a copy of the words to the song "He Is Lord" **(Reproducible 3E)**. Play the song on the **Cassette** and ask the students to follow along as they listen. Play the song again and invite them to sing.

Supplies:
Reproducible 3E, cassette player

Zillies:
Cassette

OLDER ELEMENTARY 3

Life

Choose one or more activities to bring the Bible to life.

Supplies:
chalkboard and chalk OR large piece of paper and marker

Zillies:
flying disk

Easy as Pie

Divide the students into two teams. Have them line up facing one another on opposing sides of the room. Write today's Bible verse on a chalkboard or large piece of paper:

> He (Jesus) said, "Abba, Father, for you all things are possible; remove this cup from me; yet, not what I want, but what you want."
> Mark 14:36

Place it on the wall where all the students can see it easily. Ask everyone to read the verse aloud with you. **Say: You can memorize this verse as easy as pie. Here's how.**

Show the students the **flying disk**. **Say: Teams will take turns tossing the disk back and forth to one another. If any player on your team misses the catch or drops the disk, everyone on your team has to read the Bible verse. Each time the verse is read, I will mark through one word. Each time you will have fewer and fewer words to read. Then pretty soon the verse will be unforgettable; you will be saying it without any words to read at all.**

Supplies:
cup with prayers in it

Zillies:
none

Worship

Ask the students to sit with you on the floor. **Say: Today we learned that Jesus turned to God in prayer. Jesus called God "Abba" which is Aramaic for "father." Abba was a word used by children when speaking to their father, much like us calling our fathers "daddy." Jesus trusted God completely. Today, let's go to God in prayer and show our complete trust in God. We know that God always hears our prayers. When we turn everything over to God, we can know that God will be with us and help us in the ways that God knows are best for us.**

Pass around the cup with the prayers in it. Ask each student to take one slip of paper and to hold it without reading it. **Explain: All of us will bow our heads. I will pray, "Abba, Father, we pray...." and each of you may pray silently the prayer written on your paper. After we finish praying, we will all say: Thank you, God, for hearing our prayer.**

Give each student a copy of HomeZone to enjoy this week.

Home Zone For Students

A Cup to Keep

Make a cup to keep in your room to help you remember that you can pray to God about anything. Use the following recipe three times to make three different colors of dough. Use a different color of punch mix for each recipe.

self-sealing plastic freezer bag
1 cup flour
½ cup salt
1 teaspoon cooking oil
package sugar-free powdered punch mix
1 cup hot water

Pour the flour, salt, and cooking oil into the plastic freezer bag. Seal the bag and use your fingers to knead the bag and mix the ingredients. When they are mixed well, open the bag and carefully pour in one bag of the powdered punch mix. Then add the hot water very slowly. Seal the bag again and knead until the mixture looks like a dough.

Flatten a small amount of dough with your hand. Place it on a cookie sheet. Press the open end of a large glass or can into the dough to cut out a circle. Remove the extra dough from the cookie sheet. Roll some dough between your hands to look like a rope that is about ½-inch thick. Press the fork lightly along the top of the rope. Press the rope around the edge of the dough circle. Pinch off the rope and add a coil with another color using the same process as before. Each time pinch the ends of the rope together. Continue until you have alternated colors often enough to make the cup the size you want. Pinch a small piece of the rope onto the side of the cup to make the handle.

Carefully wipe all over the outside of your cup with a damp sponge. Bake the cup in a preheated oven at 350 degrees for 40 minutes. Let the cup cool completely before you touch it.

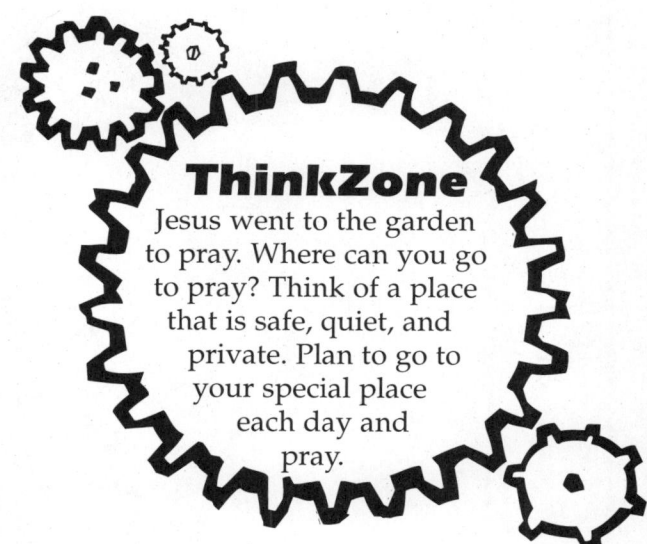

ThinkZone

Jesus went to the garden to pray. Where can you go to pray? Think of a place that is safe, quiet, and private. Plan to go to your special place each day and pray.

"Garden" Supper

Tell your family about Jesus in the garden. Ask them to help you plan a special supper using foods from a garden. You could have vegetable soup and salad with fresh strawberries for dessert. Or you could have omelettes filled with diced vegetables and pumpkin pie. What about a baked potato, green bean casserole, and carrot cake? And there is always vegetable stir-fry, rice, and fortune cookies (of course, the cookies aren't from the garden!)

Memory Verse

He (Jesus) said, "Abba, Father, for you all things are possible; remove this cup from me; yet, not what I want, but what you want."
Mark 14:36

God always hears our prayers.

Permission granted to photocopy for local church use. © 1998 Abingdon Press.

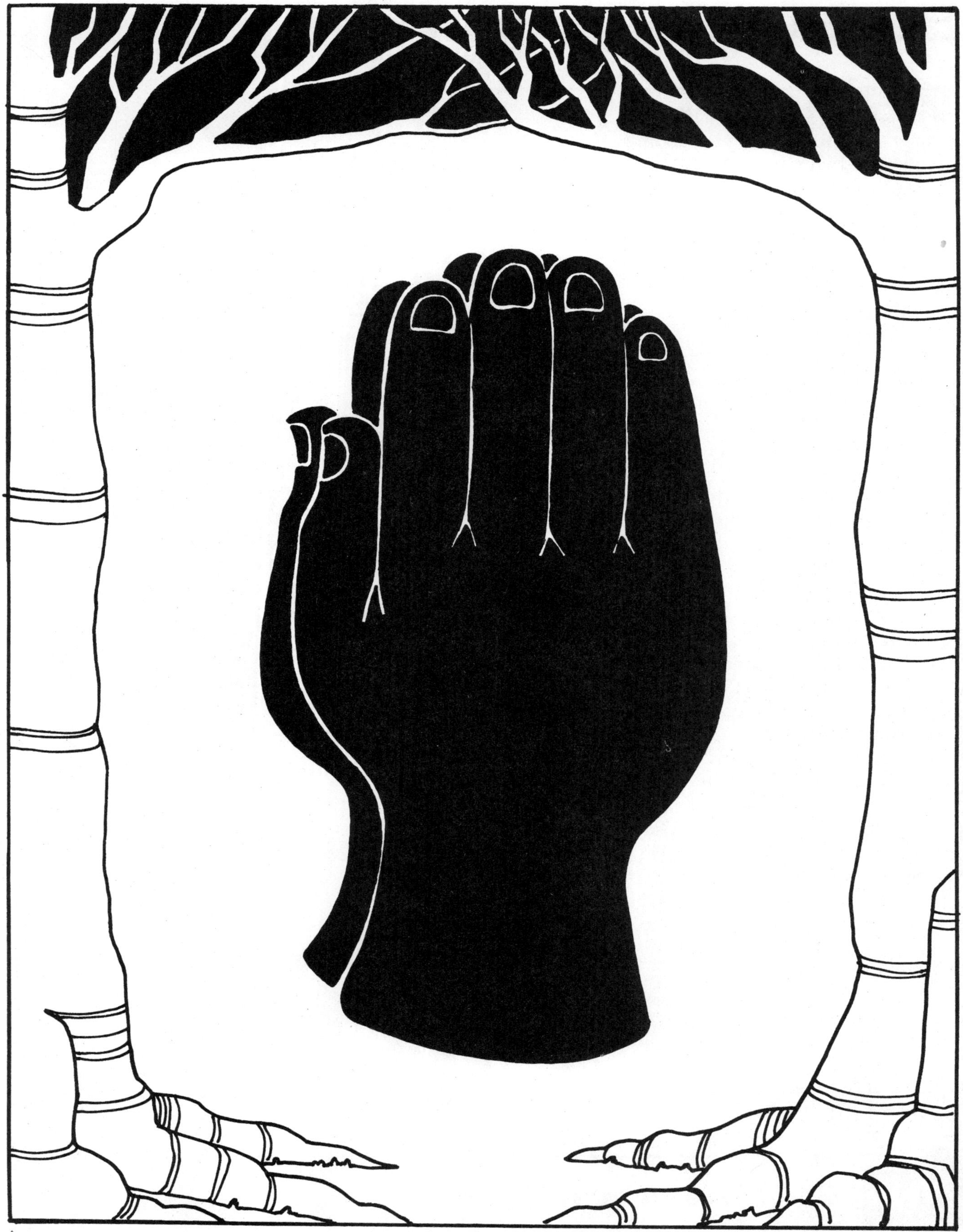

Reproducible 3D

He Is Lord

He is Lord, He is Lord.
He is risen from the dead and He is Lord.
Every knee shall bow, every tongue confess
That Jesus Christ is Lord.

He is Lord, He is Lord.
He is risen from the dead and He is Lord.
Every knee shall bow, every tongue confess
That Jesus Christ is Lord.

He is Lord, He is Lord.
He is risen from the dead and He is Lord.
Every knee shall bow, every tongue confess
That Jesus Christ is Lord.

Jesus Christ is Lord.

Arr. © 1996 New Spring Publishing, Inc. (ASCAP), admin. by Brentwood-Benson Music Publishing, Inc. All rights reserved. Used by permission.

4 Bible

Peter's Denial

Enter the

Bible Verse
I do not know this man.
   Mark 14:71

Bible Story
Matthew 26:20-25, 31-35, 69-75; Mark 14:66-72; Luke 22:54-62; John 18:15-18, 25-27; 21:15-17

After Jesus and the disciples had shared the Passover meal, they sang a hymn. After singing, Jesus told the disciples that all of them would desert him. They must have been shocked at such an idea. They were friends and followers of Jesus. But even after all the disciples pledged their loyalty to him, Jesus said that Peter would deny him three times before dawn.

In Jesus' time the Jews had adopted the Roman division of the night into four periods or watches. The first period began at six in the evening, and each period lasted three hours. The Romans had a military base at Jerusalem's Antonia Fortress; and there, between the watches, a trumpet would sound for the guards to change. The last trumpet was blown at three in the morning. The Latin word for the trumpet call was gallicinium, which means cock-crow. Some scholars suggest that it was this trumpet call that reminded Peter of his denial.

Peter may have been the most loyal of the disciples because he did follow Jesus to Caiaphas's house after Jesus was arrested. But later, when confronted, Peter was overcome with fear and denied Jesus. When Peter heard the cock-crow, he was devastated as he remembered his own cowardice.

That night must have been a turning point in Peter's life. Almost certainly it was Peter who later told others this story as an example of the forgiveness that is possible through Jesus Christ. John 21:15-17 records Jesus' appearance to Peter after the resurrection. Peter had denied Jesus three times. In this passage Jesus asks Peter three times, "Do you love me?" After Peter responds, Jesus says to Peter, "Feed my sheep." This message clearly indicates that Jesus had forgiven Peter and was asking Peter to carry on Jesus' ministry.

We can tell everyone who Jesus is.

Scope the Zone

ZONE	TIME	SUPPLIES	ZILLIES™
Zoom Into the Zone			
Get in the Zone	5 minutes	page 174, cassette player	Cassette
Who Am I?	10 minutes	page 173, pencils or pens, masking tape, small box	slide flute
BibleZone™			
Zoom Into the Bible	15 minutes	Bible for each student, Reproducible 4C, two boxes labeled "true" and "false"	sponge balls
Three of Everything	10 minutes	Reproducibles 4A and 4B	none
LifeZone			
Versatile Reversibles	10 minutes	none	flying disk, slide flute
Something to Crow About	15 minutes	Reproducible 4D, markers, scissors, glue, paper clips or coins	none
Sing	5 minutes	Reproducible 4E, cassette player	Cassette
Pray	5 minutes	none	none

Zillies™ are found in the **BibleZone™ FUNspirational™ Kit.**

OLDER ELEMENTARY 3

47

Zoom Into the Zone

Choose one or more activities to catch your children's interest.

Supplies:
page 174,
cassette player

Zillies:
Cassette

Get in the Zone

Welcome the students and let them know how happy you are to see them. Have "The Bible Zone" **(Cassette)** playing as the students enter the room, and invite them to sing with you. Have copies of the words available **(page 174)** if anyone needs them.

Supplies:
page 173,
masking tape,
pencils or pens,
small box

Zillies:
slide flute

Who Am I?

Photocopy a nametag (page 173) for each student. Have each student write his or her name on a nametag and place it in a box face down. Mix the names up. Then ask the students to stand in a circle.

Say: Everyone turn to the left. You will be facing the back of the person who was standing beside you.

Walk around the circle and let each student remove a nametag from the box and get a strip of masking tape. **Say: Please tape the nametag to the back of the person in front of you. Don't tell anyone whose name you are taping! When I use the slide flute, everyone scramble. Then you may walk around the room and ask questions to find out whose name you are wearing. Ask questions that can be answered with a yes or a no; for example, Do I have black hair? Am I wearing a blue shirt? Am I a boy? Am I a girl? You can only ask three questions from each person before you have to ask someone else. As soon as you think you know whose name you are wearing, say that person's name. If you are correct, you may have the name removed from your back and place it on the table.**

When everyone has discovered his or her identity, **say: We thought we knew each other very well. But sometimes it is hard to say who someone is. Our Bible story today tells us of Peter and the hard time he had saying who Jesus was. As a matter of fact he actually denied knowing who Jesus was.**

We can tell everyone who Jesus is.

BIBLEZONE™

Bible

Choose one or more activities to immerse your children in the Bible story.

Zoom Into the Bible

Prepare two boxes on which one has the label "True" on it and the other has the label "False" on it. Place the boxes in chairs or on the floor against a wall.

Be certain each student has a Bible. Divide the students into four teams (for ideas for creating teams, see page 167). Ask Team One to read Matthew 26:20-25, 31-35, 69-75. Ask Team Two to read Mark 14:66-73. Ask Team Three to read Luke 22:54-62. Ask Team Four to read John 18:15-18, 25-27; 21:15-17.

Have the teams line up in four lines facing the two boxes. **Say: We are going to have a "True or False Ball Blast." The first player in each line will be given a sponge ball. I will ask a question. The players should throw the balls into the boxes to show their answers—true or false. After you answer the question, go to the end of the line for your team. I will keep score to see which team gets the most correct answers.**

Be ready to give each player a **sponge ball**. If you have a large class, you may want the students to help you keep the balls rotating. The questions are on page 52 (**Reproducible 4C**). The answers are in italics.

Supplies:
Bible for each student, Reproducible 4C, two boxes labeled "true" and "false"

Zillies:
sponge balls

Three of Everything

Read or tell the story "Could It Be?" (**Reproducibles 4A and 4B**). Ask the students to follow along as you read. Suggest they echo the parts marked *echo*. (For great storytelling tips, read the article on pages 171 and 172.)

Ask: Why do you think Peter was so sure he would not ever betray Jesus? Why do you think Peter betrayed Jesus three times? How do you think Peter felt when he heard the rooster crow for the third time? Why do you think Jesus forgave Peter? Why did Jesus ask Peter three times if he loved him? What did Jesus want Peter to do when he said, "Feed my sheep"?

Supplies:
Reproducibles 4A and 4B

Zillies:
none

OLDER ELEMENTARY 3

Bible Zone Story

Could It Be?
by Michael Williams

Peter Pondered

Reclining around a table on a holy, holy night, a rabbi and his disciples talked. The rabbi stopped the conversation with a startling revelation.

"One of you will betray me,"
   he said.
"One of you will deny me,"
   he thought.
"All of you will desert me,"
   echoed his broken heart.

Those disciples who were able tried to rise above their fright. The rabbi watched as his disciples balked at the idea that one of them could hurt him—that they could betray, deny, desert him.

"One of you will betray me,"
   he said.
"One of you will deny me,"
   he thought.
"All of you will desert me,"
   echoed his broken heart.

"Could it be me?" whispered Matthew.
"Could it be me?" whimpered John.
"Could it be me?" questioned Mark.
"Could it be me?" queried Luke.
"Could it be me?" sighed Nathaniel.
"Could it be me?" doubted Thomas.
"Could it be me?" Philip asked himself.
"Could it be me?" Andrew asked his neighbor.
"Could it be me?" James asked the empty air.
"Could it be me?" uttered Bartholomew.
"Could it be me?" muttered Judas.
"It could not be me," Peter pondered.
"Which of the others?" Peter wondered.
"Before the rooster crows three times, you will say you do not know me three times," Jesus said. "For days, every time the rooster crows, you'll be reminded of the words you could not say."

One of Them

The woman approached and stared at Peter,
   "You're one of them."
The woman spoke even louder this time.
   "You're one of them."
The people around him leaned in to listen.
   "Is he one of them?"
The people around him waited to hear.
   "Is he one of them?"

No, I do not know him.
I do not know the man, I say.
Please just get out of here.
Please just go away. (echo)

The rooster crowed as if to say,
   "You're one of them."
The crowd began to grumble,
   "You're one of them."
The very night seems to question,
   "Is he one of them?"
The silence around seems to echo,
   "Is he one of them?"

No, I do not know him.
I do not know the man, I say.
Please just get out of here.
Please just go away. (echo)

Reproducible 4A
Permission granted to photocopy for local church use. © 1998 Abingdon Press.

The rooster crowed a second time,
  "You're one of them."
The woman's voice repeated,
  "You're one of them."
Peter found it hard to breathe.
  "Is he one of them?"
His sweat cut icy rivers down his neck.
  "Is he one of them?"

No, I do not know him.
I do not know the man, I say.
Please just get out of here.
Please just go away. *(echo)*

The rooster crowed once more,
  "You're one of them."
The woman's voice insisted,
  "You're one of them."
A new voice came to question.
  "Are you one of them?"
It was the voice of Jesus asking,
  "Are you one of them?"

No, I do not know him.
I do not know this Jesus, I say.
Please just let me get out of here.
Just let me go away. *(echo)*

Do You Love Me?

Called to the shore by a familiar wave.
Fed on fish by a loving hand.
Questioned by a voice he knew too well.
Will he ask if I know him now?

"Peter"—the question is harder yet,
  "Do you love me?"
"Yes, you know I love you."
  "Feed my sheep."

"Peter"—the voice is more insistent now,
  "Do you love me?"
"Yes, Lord, you know I love you."
  "Then feed my lambs."

"Peter"—the third time pierced his soul,
  "Do you love me?"
"What do I have to say? You know I love you."
  "Then be a good shepherd and feed my sheep."

Three times he said he did not know
The man to whom he longed his love to show.
"Feed my sheep" was Jesus' only command
While he fed them fish from his own hand.

"Could it be me?" we all are asking.
Could it be me he speaks to now?
Could it be me who has deserted?
Could it be me who has denied?
Could it be me who had betrayed the one
who lived and died to live again?

Could it be me he's asking,
  "Do you love me?"
Could it be me who's answering,
  "Yes"?
Could it be me he's telling,
  "Feed my lambs"?

Could be. *(echo)*
Could be. *(echo)*

Bible Zone Story

True or False Ball Blast

1. Jesus told a group of women they would betray him. *(false, he told the disciples)*

2. It was morning when Jesus said he would be betrayed. *(false, it was evening)*

3. Jesus said they would all betray him. *(false, only one would betray him)*

4. Jesus said he would be betrayed next week. *(false, that night)*

5. Jesus said he would be betrayed three times before the cock crowed. *(true)*

6. Peter was sitting in a house when he denied knowing Jesus. *(false, he was outside)*

7. All the people with Peter were warming themselves near a fire. *(true)*

8. Peter denied to a man servant that he knew Jesus. *(false, a servant girl)*

9. After Peter denied Jesus, he wept bitterly. *(true)*

10. Jesus appeared to Peter after he was raised from the dead. *(true)*

11. Jesus asked Peter four times if he loved him. *(false, three times)*

12. Jesus asked Peter to feed his lambs, sheep, and goats. *(false, just lambs and sheep)*

Reproducible 4C

Permission granted to photocopy for local church use. © 1998 Abingdon Press.

Choose one or more activities to bring the Bible to life.

Versatile Reversibles

Say: Peter was very weak when he denied knowing Jesus. When Peter realized that Jesus had forgiven him, his weakness turned into strength. Peter became one of the strongest disciples. Peter did a complete reversal.

Divide the class into two teams. Give one team the **flying disk. Say: When you are holding the disk, say a word. Toss the disk. The person on the other team who catches the disk has to say the opposite or reversal of what was just named. For example, if one player said "big," the opposing player would say "little." I will use the slide flute to signal when to begin and when to end. Play as fast as you can.**

Encourage the students to be creative. Also suggest they use words of faith: for example, believer and sinner, lost and saved, and so forth.

Supplies:
none

Zillies:
flying disk, slide flute

Something to Crow About

Give each student two copies of the rooster pattern **(Reproducible 4D),** one to cut apart and one to follow. Go over the instructions with the class carefully. If needed, show the students step by step how to create the rooster. Suggest they use bright color markers on the pieces after cutting them out and before putting them together.

Ask the students to say today's Bible verse with you: "I do not know this man" (Mark 14:71).

Say: That is what Peter said when he denied Jesus. He said it three times before the rooster crowed, just as Jesus had said he would. We use the rooster to remind us of Peter's denial. Peter loved Jesus very much, but he was too weak to stand up for Jesus and tell others about Jesus. The rooster can remind us of what happened and help us to be strong as we tell everyone about Jesus.

Supplies:
Reproducible 4D, markers, scissors, glue, paper clips or coins

Zillies:
none

 **We can tell everyone who Jesus is.**

OLDER ELEMENTARY 3

Life Zone

Choose one or more activities to bring the Bible to life.

Supplies:
Reproducible 4E, cassette player

Zillies:
Cassette

Sing

Say: Peter recognized that Jesus is the Son of God. Jesus is Lord. Because of that Peter was able to be strong and became an important leader in the church.

Give each student a copy of the words to the song "John 3:16" **(Reproducible 4E)**. Ask the students to follow along while they listen to the song on the **Cassette**. Play the song again and ask them to follow along.

Supplies:
none

Zillies:
none

Pray

Say: Peter experienced forgiveness. We can experience forgiveness too, even when we say or do things that are disappointing to us and to others. When we make mistakes, Jesus understands and forgives us. But Jesus expects us to find in his forgiveness a source of strength to help us do better the next time. Let's do a creative drama together as our prayer.

Say: I will begin by praying. When I pause, let's name a way we are weak. Then everyone hold your hand in front of your mouth and gently blow as if blowing a feather. I will continue praying. When I pause, let's name a way God helps us to be strong. Then everyone act as if you are picking up a huge, heavy boulder, lifting it over your head, and sitting it down with hardly any effort.

Pray: Dear God, we know that sometimes we make mistakes and we are weak. Sometimes we *(pause, name a weakness, then act as if blowing a feather)*. We know that you forgive us when we ask sincerely and you help us become stronger. You help us to *(pause, name a way God helps us to be strong, and then act as if moving a huge boulder)*.

Repeat the prayer and motions several times. **End by praying: Thank you, God, for forgiving us when we make mistakes. Thank you for helping us to be strong. Be with us each day as we tell others about Jesus and your love. Amen.**

Give each student a copy of HomeZone to enjoy this week.

Home Zone For Students

Rooster Glitters

Cut out the pattern of the rooster on this page. Cut a square of sandpaper that is as large as the rooster. Place the pattern on the sandpaper and draw around the pattern using a thick pencil. Use a small brush to paint white glue on the part of the rooster that you want to cover with a particular color of glitter. Sprinkle glitter over the glue. Paint glue over another part of the rooster and sprinkle on a different color of glitter. Continue doing this using different colors of glitter until the entire rooster is covered with glitter. Let it dry thoroughly.

Punch a hole near the top of the square of sandpaper. Tie thread, yarn, or ribbon through the hole. Hang the rooster in a special place.

ThinkZone
Have you ever denied something and then felt very sorry? Ask God to forgive you and help you correct your mistake. What have you learned from your mistake?

Memory Verse
I do not know this man.
Mark 14:71

Rooster Pie

Preheat your oven to 425 degrees. Combine 2 cups cooked chicken, 1 can cream of chicken soup, 1 10-ounce package of frozen peas and carrots, 2 tablespoons of minced onion, and a little salt and pepper in a bowl.

Grease a casserole dish with margarine. Pour the chicken mixture into the dish. Cover with a ready-made pie crust. Bake in the oven for 25 to 30 minutes until the crust is lightly browned.

We can tell everyone who Jesus is.

Song Zone

John 3:16

John 3:16
Says that God so loved the world
He gave His only begotten Son
That whoever believes in Him
Will never die but have eternal life
(Repeat)

He is the Way
He is the Truth
He is the Life
So put your faith in Jesus Christ
And your soul will never die

You'll never die...never die
You'll have eternal life
Forever and ever.

John 3:16
Says that God so loved the world
He gave His only begotten Son
That whoever believes in Him
Will never die but have eternal life
(Repeat)

He is the Way
He is the Truth
He is the Life
So put your faith in Jesus Christ
And your soul will never die

You'll never die...never die
You'll have eternal life
Forever and ever.
(Repeat)

Arr. © 1995 Bridge Building Music, Inc. (BMI), admind. by Brentwood-Benson Music Publishing, Inc. All rights reserved. Used by permission.

Reproducible 4E

Permission granted to photocopy for local church use. © 1998 Abingdon Press.

5 Bible Zone

To the Crucifixion

Enter the Zone

Bible Verse
"Truly this man was God's Son!"
Mark 15:39b

Bible Story
Matthew 26:36-50, 56b; 27:27-32, 57-58; Mark 15:39;
Luke 22:39-47; 23:26, 33-34, 46;
John 18:1-8, 28-40; 19:6-8, 13-16; 19:31-37

Many people played important roles in the days leading to the crucifixion of Jesus. Judas betrayed Jesus. A crowd sent by the chief priests seized Jesus in the garden. The Sanhedrin tried Jesus. Witnesses lied about Jesus. The crowd demanded that Jesus be crucified.

In the time of Jesus, Jews had authority to arrest and examine but not to sentence or execute persons who were accused of sedition or insurrection. Only the Roman government could carry out the sentence. Pilate was the Roman procurator of Jerusalem, and he was in the city to handle difficulties that might arise as the Jews celebrated Passover. When Jesus was brought before Pilate, Jesus was accused of seditious activity, of encouraging the people not to pay their taxes to Caesar, and of assuming the title of king.

The political crime of insurrection was punishable by death. Jesus was accused of claiming to be King of the Jews. This claim made Jesus a threat to the Roman emperor. But Pilate couldn't find sufficient evidence to justify crucifixion. The angry crowd, agitated by the chief priests, demanded the release of a convicted murderer, Barabbas, and the death of Jesus.

At last Pilate gave in to the desires of the crowd. Jesus was killed by crucifixion. Crucifixion was intended to reduce crime by the public shame and horror attached to the cross. The arms of the victim were stretched out and lashed or nailed to a crossbeam, which was then nailed or lashed to a vertical pole. Death was an agonizingly slow process involving exposure to extremes of weather, hunger, thirst, and exhaustion.

During such agony Jesus said, "Father, forgive them; for they do not know what they are doing" (Luke 23:34). This remarkable forgiveness is accompanied by the deep trust of his dying words: "Father, into your hands I commend my spirit" (Luke 23:46).

The cross has become a symbol that reminds us of God's great love for us as shown through Jesus Christ.

God loves us so much that God's Son, Jesus, died for us.

Scope the Zone

ZONE	TIME	SUPPLIES	⊚ ZILLIES™
Zoom Into the Zone			
Get in the Zone	5 minutes	page 174, cassette player	Cassette
Rejection Replay	15 minutes	box or basket	sponge balls, slide flute
Music Moves	5 minutes	cassette player	Cassette, hose
BibleZone™			
Zoom Into the Bible	15 minutes	Bible for each student, masking tape	none
Hear the Bible Story	10 minutes	Reproducibles 5A, 5B, and 5C	none
Battle Ball	10 minutes	masking tape, several brooms	sponge balls, slide flute
LifeZone			
The Darkest Day	10 minutes	Bible, Reproducible 5D, white or yellow crayons, diluted black tempera paint, brushes, bowls	none
Sing and Worship	5 minutes	Reproducible 5E, cassette player	Cassette

⊚ Zillies™ are found in the **BibleZone™ FUNspirational™ Kit.**

OLDER ELEMENTARY 3

Zoom Into the Zone

Choose one or more activities to catch your children's interest.

Supplies:
page 174,
cassette player

Zillies:
Cassette

Get in the Zone

Welcome the students and let them know how happy you are to see them. Have "The Bible Zone" **(Cassette)** playing and invite the students to sing with you. Have copies of the words **(page 174)** available.

Supplies:
box or basket

Zillies:
sponge balls
slide flute

Rejection Replay

Select one student to be Jesus. Ask all the other students to stand in a line facing Jesus. Tell them they will be the Sanhedrin. **Say: The Sanhedrin was a council of men who thought Jesus was guilty of blasphemy because Jesus claimed to be the Messiah. They did not like what Jesus said, and they rejected him.**

Place a box or basket near Jesus that contains all of the **sponge balls**. Ask the members of the Sanhedrin to stand with their legs spread apart. **Say: Jesus will try to throw the balls through your legs. You may bend over and catch the balls and thrown them back. If a ball goes between the legs of any member of the Sanhedrin, that person becomes Jesus, and the game begins again.** Use the **slide flute** to signal the beginning of the game.

Say: Just like the person playing Jesus continued to throw the balls in this game, Jesus continued to preach and teach. Eventually the rejection became so strong that Jesus was arrested, tried, and crucified. We will learn more about that today.

Supplies:
cassette player

Zillies:
Cassette,
hose

Music Moves

Have the students stand in a circle facing one another. Give each student one of the **hose**. **Say: Slip one one end of the hose over your left hand. Take the other end of a hose from the person standing across from you and put that end over your right hand.** Practice the following motions: Right hand up. Right hand down. Left hand up. Left hand down. Both hands up. Turn around (where they are standing). Both hands down. Right hand up. Right hand down. Left hand up. Left hand down. Both hands up. Turn around. Both hands down. Repeat from beginning.

Play "There's Power in the Blood" **(Cassette)** and lead the students in the motions listed above. Use two smaller circles if you have a large class.

Bible

Choose one or more activities to immerse your children in the Bible story.

Zoom Into the Bible

Supplies:
Bible for each student, masking tape

Zillies:
none

Use masking tape to prepare a playing area that looks like a large tic-tacktoe grid on the floor. You will need nine spaces large enough for the students to stand on.

Divide the class into two teams, the Xs and the Os. Ask the teams to stand in two lines facing one another on opposite sides of the playing area. **Explain: We will play this game like ticktacktoe. I will ask a question. You will need to look in your Bibles for the answer. The first player on either team to give the correct answer gets to stands on any square. If the answer is not correct, the question is open for anyone on the opposite team to answer. If no one answers, I will go to the next question. The first team to get three players standing in a row wins.**

Give the following instructions and questions:
1. Read Matthew 26:36. Where did Jesus go and what was he going to do there? *(Gethsemane, pray)*
2. Read Matthew 26:39. What did Jesus pray? *(Remove this cup from me, yet not what I want, but what you want.)*
3. Read Matthew 26:38-45. Each time that Jesus went to the disciples, he found them doing what? *(sleeping)*
4. Read Luke 22:41-44. What happened as Jesus prayed? *(He prayed more earnestly, and his sweat fell like drops of blood.)*
5. Read Matthew 26:47. What was used as a sign to betray Jesus? *(a kiss)*
6. Read John 18:33. What did Pilate ask Jesus? *(Are you the King of the Jews?)*
7. Read John 18:40. Who did the crowd demand to be released? *(Barabbas)*
8. Read Matthew 27:32. Who carried the cross for Jesus? *(Simon of Cyrene)*
9. Read Matthew 27:33. Where was the cross carried and what was the meaning of the name of the place? *(Golgotha, which means Place of a Skull)*
10. Read Luke 23:34. What words did Jesus say while on the cross? *(Father, forgive them; for they do not know what they are doing.)*
11. Read Mark 15:39b. What did the centurion say after Jesus died? *("Truly this man was God's Son!")*

 **God loves us so much that God's Son, Jesus, died for us.**

BibleZone activities are continued on page 65.

Bible Zone Story

Trees of Sorrow, Trees of Hope

by Michael Williams

The Olive Tree

I am older than memory, almost older than time. I have stood in this garden until I am gnarled and twisted with the years. I am years beyond bearing fruit, and any beauty I might have possessed in my youth is gone. I still do provide shade for the weary traveler and a place for the birds to roost. I have seen many things in my time and have weathered many storms. Oh, the stories I could tell you.

For example, last night a rabbi came with his disciples to pray in my garden. It is a powerful thing to overhear the prayers of another soul. As this teacher prayed, he wept and sweated what at first appeared to be sweat; but as I looked closer, I saw that they were really beads of blood. He prayed again and again that a cup would pass him by. I do not know what cup he was speaking about, but it must have had a very bitter drink inside. Then he began to pray that God's will be done. He prayed that over and over. Several times he rose to check on his disciples, but they were always asleep. This didn't just happen once but several times. They seemed to be completely unable to understand what he must be going through. Those sleepyheads clearly disappointed their teacher, but he simply returned to his prayers.

After a long time a man came into the garden, looking around as if he were searching for someone. When he saw the rabbi, the man approached and greeted him by kissing him on the cheek. I thought at first they were good friends, until I saw the soldiers and guards emerge from the shadows to arrest the teacher. It was the most remarkable thing. He wouldn't let his disciples protect him. I do not know whether this was because he didn't think they would be much help or if this was the bitter cup he was talking to God about.

I do not know what terrible things he will have to face. When you have been around as long as I have, you have seen most of the terrors life has to offer. All I know is that after their teacher was taken away, his sleepy students woke up long enough to run in all directions. Believe me, I have seen enough to know that no matter how many friends and followers desert him, that rabbi will never be alone.

Reproducible 5A

Permission granted to photocopy for local church use. © 1998 Abingdon Press.

ilate's Table

I am nothing to Pilate, just something to put his scrolls on or to hold a cup or to lean upon when he is tired of standing. He is not even here most of the time. He spends as many days as possible at Caesarea by the Sea. The weather is better there, and it's more like the Roman cities he is used to. He only comes to Jerusalem when there might be trouble.

On the really important religious holidays people always get stirred up. That's especially true on Passover. That is when the Jewish people remember the time their God freed them from being slaves in Egypt. Whenever they start telling stories about gaining their freedom from the Egyptians, they also will start thinking about freedom from the Romans. That's usually when the trouble starts.

This year the troublemaker seems to be strangely quiet—a man named Jesus. He came before Pilate because they say he claimed to be King of the Jews. You see, Caesar doesn't like any other kings around that he can't control. I could tell right off that Pilate felt that it was a waste of his time to even talk to this Jesus. He asked if this fellow thought he was a king, and the stranger gave the strangest answer. He said, "You say so." It was as if Pilate's reading the charge meant that he thought Jesus was a king. I have been Pilate's table long enough to know that he didn't mean anything like that.

The quiet man continued, "My kingdom is not like a kingdom in this world, because it is not of this world. I came to be a witness to the truth." I thought to myself, *You had better worry about being a better witness for yourself.* Pilate didn't seem to know what to say at first, then he sputtered, "What is truth?" Then Pilate went outside to talk to the crowd gathered there. I could hear a lot of shouting, but I couldn't make out many of the words. Two jumped out at me, though.

One was "crucify" and the other was the name "Barabbas." Catching just those two words, I decided that Pilate had given the crowd a choice and they had decided for this Jesus and against Barabbas.

But I was wrong. When Pilate returned, he was clearly irritated. He just wanted the trial to be over and the matter settled. He wanted to get back to more enjoyable activities like eating and conversation with other Romans. So he sent Jesus to his death. Then Pilate sat on me for the longest time after everyone else was gone. I can tell you from long experience, it felt like the weight of the world was on him and on me.

Bible 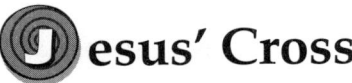 Story

Jesus' Cross

When I was a young sapling, all I ever wanted was to grow straight and tall. When the wind would blow and other young trees would bend, I would stiffen myself and try my best to stand up straight. I wanted people to notice me and comment on my height and my straightness. Sure enough, they did. One day a group of woodcutters came by and commented on me. I just beamed and stood even straighter. What I didn't realize was that they didn't just want to admire me. No, they were going to cut me down.

It was a nightmare, I can tell you. Falling my full length to the earth, then being dragged by teams of oxen to a place where I had my bark stripped off and my length, of which I was so proud, was cut into two pieces. The two pieces were fitted together with notches, one across the other. Then I was given to a man to drag through the streets of a city.

This man was so hurt and tired that he could hardly lift me. His back was bleeding from the lashes of a whip, and he wore a crown made of thorns. After he fell with me, a tall man with skin as dark as the deepest shadows of the forest lifted me and carried me the rest of the way to a hill that looked for all the world like a human skull.

When we arrived at the hill, they laid me down and placed the bleeding man on top of me. I thought at first that I was going to be some new sort of bed on which he could rest. Then the soldiers who had accompanied us took large metal spikes, and with a short-handled hammer drove them between the man's wrist bones and into me. Then they drove other spikes through his feet and afterwards lifted me up and set me in a hole, so I was standing straight and tall again.

But I was no longer proud, since I had finally realized what a terrible purpose I had been used for. The man kept pulling his weight up by the spikes in his wrists so he could take a breath. Then he would let himself down because it hurt so badly, I suppose. They stabbed him in the side, I guess to make him die quicker.

He cried out several times. The most startling thing I heard him say, though, was to forgive the people who had done this to him because they didn't know what they were doing. Then he stopped pulling up, which meant he stopped breathing. Some people came and got him down and took him away.

I never saw him again after that day, but I hope his word of forgiveness included me. If I had known how I would be used, I never would have tried so hard to grow straight and tall. You see, I didn't know what I was doing, either.

Reproducible 5C

Permission granted to photocopy for local church use. © 1998 Abingdon Press.

Bible Zone

Choose one or more activities to immerse your children in the Bible story.

Hear the Bible Story

Supplies: Reproducibles 5A, 5B, and 5C

Zillies: none

Plan to read or tell the three parts of the story "Trees of Sorrow, Trees of Hope" **(Reproducibles 5A, 5B, and 5C)**. Or ask three students who are dramatic readers to read the story for everyone. You may also want to invite a guest storyteller to tell this dramatic story.

Ask: How do you think the disciples felt, knowing that they had been sleeping when Jesus had asked them to stay awake? when Jesus was arrested and taken away? How do you think Pilate felt when he knew he had condemned an innocent man to his death? Imagine you were at the Crucifixion. How do you think the people felt who witnessed the death of Jesus?

Battle Ball

Supplies: masking tape, several brooms

Zillies: sponge balls, slide flute

Place a long strip of masking tape down the center of the floor. Have a broom for each student. **Say: The Sanhedrin could not give Jesus a trial because he did not commit blasphemy or break a religious law. The Sanhedrin did not give up, though. They had Jesus taken to Pilate to be tried for a political crime. Jesus was accused of claiming to be the King of the Jews, but even Pilate could not find evidence to prove that Jesus should be crucified. So Pilate went to the crowd and let them make the decision for him.**

Divide the class into two teams—Pilate's team and the Sanhedrin's team. If you do not have a broom for each player, the game can be played in sets. Have the players hold their brooms and stand opposite one another with the masking tape between them. **Say: I will toss the sponge balls down the line. Your job is to keep the sponge ball off of your side and on the side of the opposing team. I will use the slide flute to signal when to stop. The team with the fewest balls on its side wins.**

 **God loves us so much that God's Son, Jesus, died for us.**

OLDER ELEMENTARY 3

65

Life

Choose one or more activities to bring the Bible to life.

Supplies:
Bible, Reproducible 5D, white or yellow crayons, diluted black tempera paint, brushes, bowls

Zillies:
none

The Darkest Day

Ask a student to read Mark 15:33-39 to everyone. **Say: When Jesus died, the sky turned dark. One of the people witnessing the Crucifixion was a Roman centurion who was there to act as guard. The centurion, a Roman soldier and a Gentile, stood at the foot of the cross and recognized that Jesus is the Son of God. This revelation of the centurion tells us that the good news was for the whole world, not just for the Jewish people. Jesus died for everyone. Jesus died for you and me.**

Give each student a copy of the art of the three crosses **(Reproducible 5D)**. Ask the students to read aloud together today's Bible verse that is printed on the picture. Suggest they use white or yellow crayons to outline the verse and the crosses. Then suggest they cover the entire picture with diluted black tempera paint. The white or yellow will show through. Let the pictures dry.

Say: The darkest day was the day that Jesus died. But now we have light because Jesus died for us.

 **God loves us so much that God's Son, Jesus, died for us.**

Supplies:
Reproducible 5E, cassette player

Zillies:
Cassette

Sing and Worship

Give each student a copy of the words to the song "For Me" **(Reproducible 5E)**. Play the song on the **Cassette** and ask the students to follow along. Play the song again and invite them to sing with you. Ask them to sing with an attitude of praise and worship.

Ask the students to say today's Bible verse with you: "Truly this man was God's Son!" (Mark 15:39b). **Pray: Dear God, thank you for your Son, Jesus Christ. Thank you for your great love that saved us through Jesus' death. We know that Jesus died for each of us. Be with us now and always. Help each of us live according to your will. We love you, God. Amen.**

Give each student a copy of HomeZone to enjoy this week.

BibleZone™

Home Zone For Students

Nail It Down

The earliest nails were made of bone, wood, or stone. Eventually they were made from iron or bronze. It is said that the nails used to build Solomon's Temple were made of gold.

The Romans used nails made from iron to nail their victims to the cross. Nails were driven through the hands and feet of the person being crucified; then they were left there to die.

Nails remind us of the horrible suffering Jesus experienced. They have become an important Christian symbol of hope and resurrection. Often nails are put together in the form of a cross.

You can make a cross necklace to wear or hang in your room. Flat nails with blunt ends (such as concrete nails) have a unique look and are neat to use. Lay them together in the form of a cross. Use contact cement to glue them together where they intersect. You will need a length of yarn or leather cord. Beginning in the middle of the cord, wrap the cord around the cross section of the nails a couple of times. Then tie the ends of the cord together.

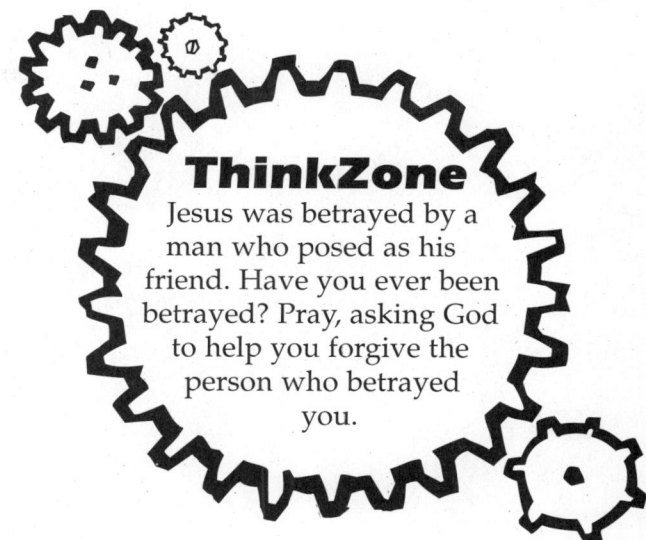

ThinkZone

Jesus was betrayed by a man who posed as his friend. Have you ever been betrayed? Pray, asking God to help you forgive the person who betrayed you.

Good Friday Breakfast

You will need:
12 slices of bread
12 eggs
salt and pepper
6 teaspoons of butter or margarine

Preheat your oven to 350 degrees. Grease a 12-cup muffin tin. Remove the crust from the bread. Place one bread slice in each muffin cup and push it down gently so that it looks like a cup with four corners.

Drop a small, raw egg in each cup. Sprinkle with salt and pepper. Top each with ½ teaspoon butter. Bake for 15 minutes or until the eggs are cooked and the bread is toasted. This will be enough to feed six people. You can make fewer servings if you do not need so many.

Serve your breakfast with your favorite juice and sliced fruit.

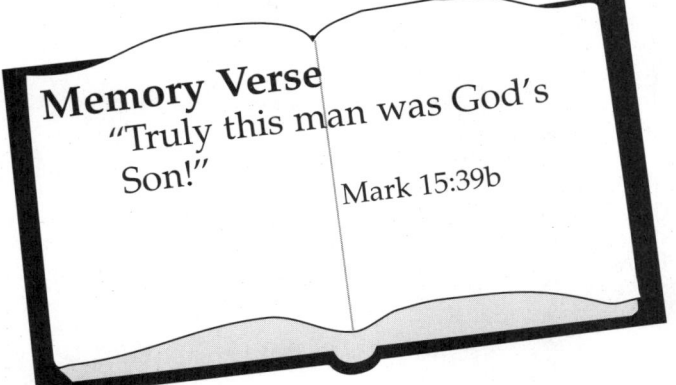

Memory Verse
"Truly this man was God's Son!" Mark 15:39b

God loves us so much that God's Son, Jesus, died for us.

Permission granted to photocopy for local church use. © 1998 Abingdon Press.

Song Zone

For Me

See him dying on a tree;
can it be he dies for me?
Never thought that I would see,
such as this for me.

As the Father looks upon
this, His only, dying, Son,
sees He now the work is done,
finished now for me.

For this moment he was born
long ago on Christmas morn.
Dying, he fulfilled God's plan,
paying for the sins of man.

Heaven's gates are opened wide,
for the blood has been applied.
I shall one day stand inside,
when he comes for me.

Words by Herb Owen
© 1988 New Spring Publishing, Inc. (ASCAP), a division of Brentwood-Benson Music Publishing, Inc., All rights reserved. Used by permission.

Reproducible 5E
Permission granted to photocopy for local church use. © 1998 Abingdon Press.

6 Bible Zone

The Resurrection

Enter the Zone

Bible Verse
He is not here; for he has been raised.
Matthew 28:6a

Bible Story
Matthew 28:1-10; Mark 16:1-8; Luke 24:1-12; John 20:1-10

The events surrounding the Crucifixion and the Resurrection were viewed and experienced differently by the different persons involved. The Scriptures tell us that Jesus faced trial and crucifixion alone. All Jesus' disciples ran away when the crowd came to the Garden of Gethsemane to arrest him. While the Sanhedrin tried Jesus, Peter was near; but three times he denied knowing Jesus. The crowd demanded crucifixion. Not a single disciple stepped from the crowd to support Jesus. No one rushed forward to carry the heavy cross for his beloved friend.

Many members of the Council, which was the Jewish governing body and highest court, were threatened by Jesus' ministry, and their response was to kill Jesus. However, Joseph of Arimathea was also on the Council, and his actions showed that he did not feel threatened by Jesus. Joseph responded to the horror of the Crucifixion by asking Pilate for the body. He saved it from the indignity of being left to decompose on the hill, a practice not uncommon to the Romans.

The four Gospel accounts vary some about the exact time in the morning, how many people went to the tomb, what was seen, what was spoken, and so forth (see Matthew 28, Mark 16, and Luke 24). All accounts agree that women first discovered the empty tomb.

The Scriptures tell us that the women were the only followers who stayed with Jesus. They were at the Crucifixion, and only these women came to the tomb to prepare the body of Jesus for proper burial.

The Resurrection is central to our faith as Christians. Through the Resurrection, God's intention became clear—Jesus is the Christ. "If Christ has not been raised, your faith is futile and you are still in your sins" (1 Corinthians 15:17). Our understanding of the Resurrection is surrounded by joy and mystery. No one witnessed Jesus rising from the dead. Our faith enables us to accept the mystery and praise God for it.

Jesus is alive!

Scope the Zone

ZONE	TIME	SUPPLIES	ZILLIES™
Zoom Into the Zone			
Get in the Zone	5 minutes	page 174, cassette player	Cassette
Eggstra Effort	10 minutes	four spoons	butterfly beanbag, rubber egg balls, slide flute
BibleZone™			
Zoom Into the Bible	15 minutes	Bible for each student	none
Easter Trope	10 minutes	Reproducibles 6A and 6B	none
LifeZone			
Great Eggs	20 minutes	Reproducibles 6C and 6D, uncooked eggs, short candle, pencils and small nails, Easter egg dyes, jars, spoons, cotton swabs	none
Butterfly Puzzler	15 minutes	Reproducible 6C, marker, Bibles	slide flute
Sing	5 minutes	Reproducible 6E, cassette player	Cassette
Butterfly Feet?	10 minutes	white paper, pencils, paint, crayons, markers, OR glue and glitter	none
Sign 'n Pray	5 minutes	none	none

Zillies™ are found in the **BibleZone™ FUNspirational™ Kit.**

OLDER ELEMENTARY 3

Zoom Into the Zone

Choose one or more activities to catch your children's interest.

Supplies:
page 174, cassette player

Zillies:
Cassette

Get in the Zone

Welcome each student with a smile. **Say: Today is a day of new beginnings! Jesus is alive! Today we hear the wonderful story of the Resurrection.**

Play "The Bible Zone" **(Cassette)**. Invite the students to sing along with you. Provide copies of the words **(page 174)** to anyone who needs them.

Supplies:
four spoons

Zillies:
butterfly beanbag, rubber egg balls, slide flute

Eggstra Effort

Say: Today we will learn about the Resurrection. Jesus lived; Jesus died; Jesus was raised from the dead and lives again. We often think of new life when we hear about the Resurrection. Because of Jesus we all have new life.

Show the students the **rubber egg balls** and the **butterfly beanbag**. **Say: The butterfly and the egg are both symbols of new life.**

Divide the students into two teams and have them line up side by side on one end of the room. Give the first player of each team two spoons and two rubber egg balls. Place the butterfly beanbag across the room from the students.

Explain: This is a relay race that takes "eggstra" effort. You will carry the rubber egg balls in your spoons across the room. When you reach the butterfly beanbag, put down your spoons, pick up the butterfly beanbag, "fly" it around while you turn in a circle, put the butterfly beanbag back down, pick up the spoons, carry them back across the room, and tag the next player on your team. Then that player does everything you just did. The team that has all its players go through the race first is the winner.

Use the **slide flute** to signal when to begin.

Jesus is alive!

BibleZone™

Bible

Choose one or more activities to immerse your children in the Bible story.

Zoom Into the Bible

Be sure each student has a Bible. Divide the students into teams. Ask Team One to read Matthew 28:1-10. Ask Team Two to read Mark 16:1-8. Ask Team Three to read Luke 24:1-12. Ask Team Four to read John 20:1-10.

Talk with the students about the events of the Resurrection. **Say: The four Gospel accounts vary some about the exact time in the morning, how many people went to the tomb, what was seen, and what was spoken. Ask: What do all four accounts agree on?** (*Women first discovered the empty tomb.*)

Say: The disciples saw Jesus crucified. They watched in horror as he suffered and died. Jesus' body was taken from the cross and placed in a tomb. Can you imagine how devastated the disciples must have felt. Can you imagine how they must have cried? Then, on the third day after his death, Jesus appeared to those who loved him. The good news spread throughout! Their sorrow turned to complete joy! After the Resurrection the disciples preached and taught others about their risen Lord and Savior, Jesus Christ.

Supplies:
Bible for each student

Zillies:
none

Easter Trope

Read or tell the story "Whom Do You Seek?" **(Reproducibles 6A and 6B).** Talk with the students about the meaning of a trope (see the italicized information at the top of **Reproducible 6A**). (For great storytelling tips, read the article on pages 171 and 172.)

Ask: What Scripture was the play referring to? (*John 20:15*)

Say: The Resurrection is surrounded with mystery and joy. No one saw Jesus rise from the dead. There were no witnesses. But Jesus appeared to his followers on the third day, and he was alive! Our faith enables us to believe in the Resurrection as God's power to change death into life. Jesus was victorious over evil and death. Jesus died, he was buried, and he rose from the dead.

Supplies:
Reproducibles 6A and 6B

Zillies:
none

OLDER ELEMENTARY 3

Bible Zone Story

Whom Do You Seek?
by Michael Williams

During the Middle Ages the Church began to do short plays based on Bible stories. Most people could not read and write, so these plays helped them learn the stories of their faith. Often priests and lay brothers from religious orders played all the parts, even those of women. Our earliest drama is a brief dialogue called a trope and was probably sung. Perhaps the most famous trope was based on the Easter story and was called "Quem quaeritis," which means "Whom do you seek?"

I was just a boy when one of the older brothers took me aside one day and told me that I was to have a part in the Easter play. I was only nine years old at the time and had seen the play only three times. I came to live at the monastery when I was six, and my parents left me there to be schooled and to become a monk after a time.

Several days later I learned that I was to be one of the two men dressed in white at the tomb. We all gathered on Ash Wednesday with crosses made of ashes placed between and above our eyebrows to learn what our roles would require of us. It was then that I learned that, at my young age, I would be the young man in white robes who spoke. I was still learning to read myself, so an older brother was assigned to rehearse me on the lines he had learned in the same way over half a century earlier. He taught me the tune of the chant to which I would sing the words.

Every day he would repeat the line that came just before mine, prompting me to say my character's lines. I began my part with the question, "Whom do you seek?" When they answer me that they "seek Jesus who was crucified and buried," I am to ask them, "Why do you seek the living among the dead?" You see, my whole part was made up of questions. When the others express that what I said might be true, I am to ask, "Did he not tell you that he was going before you into Galilee?"

We went over and over these lines until I could say them in my sleep. In fact, they sounded like I was singing them in my sleep. Finally, the older brother asked me, "Do you have any idea what you are saying?"

I confessed that I did not have the slightest idea what I was saying, so he began to teach me the meaning of the words. "What I am about to tell you is a great mystery. Your head may not understand it all; but if you listen with your heart, you will enter into the Mystery, and living there you will become a different person."

So he told me the story of Jesus' cruel death at the hands of religious leaders. He told me of the forgiveness Jesus offered to those who nailed him to the cross. He told me of the followers of Jesus, the men who ran away and the women who stayed close by. He spoke of the man who gave a tomb for Jesus' body, the women who prepared his body for burial, and how the coming of the Jewish Sabbath had stopped them in the middle of their preparations. He spoke of their return to the tomb to find it empty and of my part in telling them that it was empty, that Jesus was risen and gone. Of course, I had heard all this read in the Latin of the Bible, but never heard it told right out the way this brother spoke it. It was like

Reproducible 6A
Permission granted to photocopy for local church use. © 1998 Abingdon Press.

I was there watching myself. I did listen with my heart, and I did become a part of the story.

Was I different afterwards? Well, my singing of my lines was different. The older brother heard it right away. "Sing the Mystery," he would repeat. "Sing the Mystery."

As the days passed, I was taught how Jesus' disciples hid out in fear for their lives. Then Jesus appeared to them all but Thomas; a week later he appeared to Thomas as well. Jesus ate fish by the Sea of Galilee with them. Jesus asked Peter three times if he loved him, and then told him to feed his sheep and lambs as a sign of that love. These events somehow turned the fumbling, mistaken followers into people who would risk their lives to tell the story I would sing in the Easter service. And all this was recorded in the Holy Gospels.

Then he told me that, though the Bible did not mention it, he had heard that Thomas had gone as far as India to tell of Jesus. He said that Peter had been crucified upside down, because he didn't feel worthy to die in the same manner as his teacher. This mystery we call resurrection had changed those disciples of old into different people. I knew somewhere deep in my bones that the story I was to help tell could do that still.

The day came for our trope to be performed. The first service of Easter I sat robed in white next to the tomb that had been made by the carpenter brothers for us. As the others approached, I sang, "Whom do you seek, O mortals?"

They answered, "Jesus, who was crucified, O heavenly being."

I responded, "Why do you seek the living among the dead? He is not here. He is risen, and went before you as he said."

The trope was over so quickly that it hardly seemed that it really had happened. That must have been the way the first disciples felt when they received that news so good it couldn't help but be true. They wondered and doubted and were filled with fear, we are told.

I understood why they would feel that way and perhaps imagine that it hadn't happened at all. Out of such doubt and fear and questioning, true faith is born. And it is only proven by those stories that are so filled with wonder that we can hardly believe them. I was fortunate to have learned that so young. Some never learn it, even here among the brothers.

Now I am the older brother, and that first Easter trope seems like it was a lifetime ago, which it was. I have begun training the child who will ask the questions that will call forth the mystery this next Easter. Can I do for him what the older brother did for me? I do not know.

I have learned that listening with the heart is a gift from God. I cannot plant a listening seed in another, nor can I make it grow. God sows the listening seed in the heart, and I water it and watch in wonder as it comes to bear fruit. I will simply tell the stories that were told to me, and teach the notes as well as the words that carry that mystery we call resurrection from one to another. Then I will tell him, as I was told, "Sing the Mystery."

And so I say to you, my friends, in your life and in your song, "Sing the Mystery. Sing the Mystery."

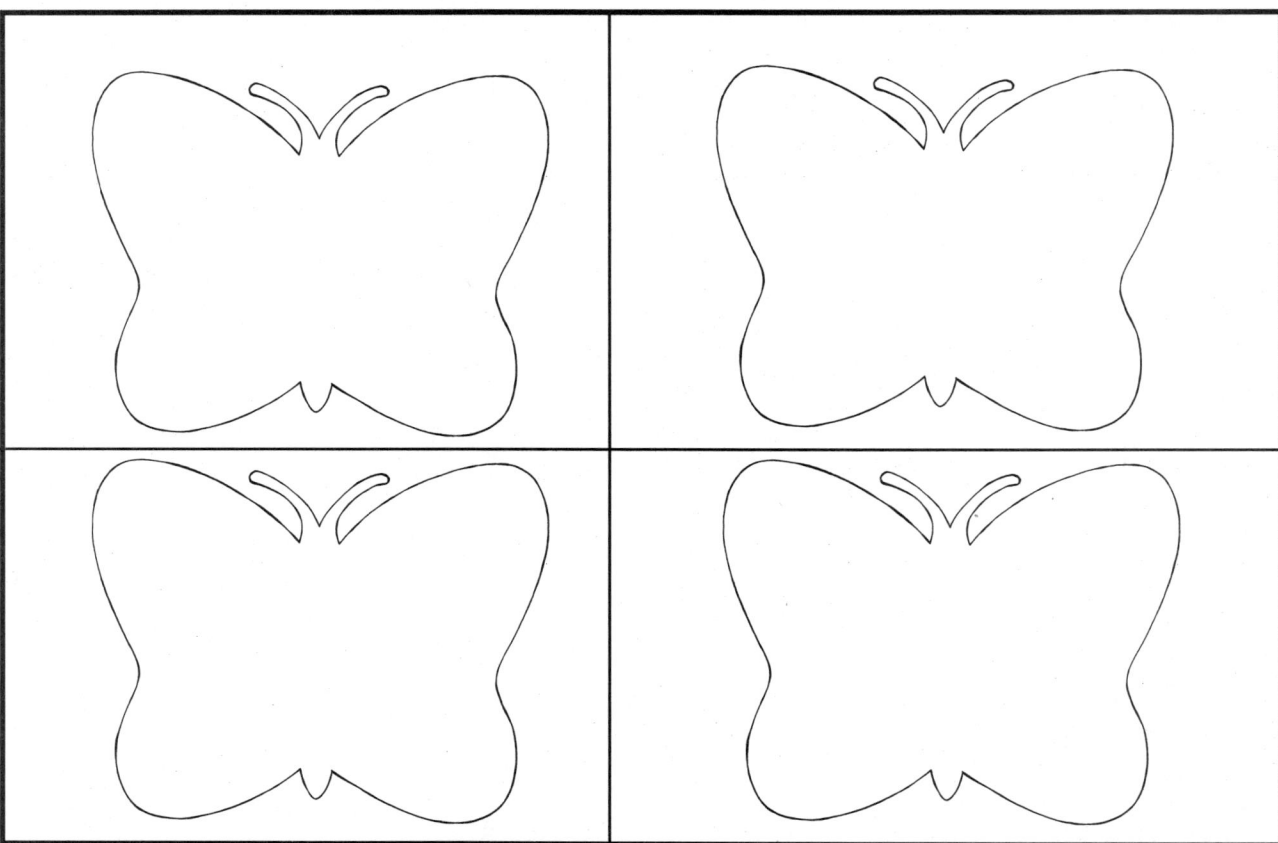

Pysanka Eggs

You will need eggs that have not been boiled, a short candle, powdered dyes in several colors (you can use Easter egg dyes), cotton swabs, and a kistka. To make a kistka, push a small nail into the eraser end of a pencil.

Prepare the powdered dyes in jars. Light the candle and hold the nail of the kistka over the flame to heat the nail. Dip the nail end into the melted wax of the candle and draw on the egg with the wax. Do this again several times. Everywhere you put wax will be white on the egg.

Then use a spoon to dip the egg into the lightest color of dye you have. Hold the egg in the dye for five minutes. Then remove the egg and let it dry for a few minutes. Use the nail of the kistka to apply wax to all of the areas that you want to remain the color of the dye you just used.

Dip the egg in the dye that is the second lightest color you have. Hold the egg there for five minutes, then remove it and let it dry for five minutes. Use the nail end of the kistka to apply wax to all the areas of the egg that you want to remain the second color.

Repeat the process, each time using the color that is next in order from light to dark. Let your egg dry.

You can keep your egg for a long time if you "blow it out." To do that, use a needle or pin to put a small hole in one end. Make a larger hole in the other end. Cut a straw to make a shorter straw, about three inches long. Put the straw over the small hole and blow hard. The egg will drain from the larger hole.

Tie a knot in one end of a piece of ribbon. Thread the other end of the ribbon onto a large needle. Put the needle through the holes of the egg so that the knot is at the bottom of the egg. Remove the needle and tie a knot at the top of the egg. You can hang your pysanka egg and enjoy it at Easter and all year long.

Life

Choose one or more activities to bring the Bible to life.

Great Eggs

Say: Pysanka eggs were first made in the Ukraine, a country beside Russia. They were made at Easter as a way to recognize the new life that God has given us. Pysanka eggs are beautifully decorated with wax and different colors of dye.

Give each student a copy of the pysanka pattern **(Reproducible 6D)** and the instructions **(bottom half, Reproducible 6C)**. This project takes time and may be worked on between other activities, or you may prefer to have the students make them at home.

Supplies: Reproducibles 6C and 6D, uncooked eggs, short candle, pencils and small nails, Easter egg dyes, jars, spoons, cotton swabs optional: pin or needle, ribbon

Zillies: none

Butterfly Puzzler

Make six copies of the butterfly cards **(top half, Reproducible 6C)**. Cut out the pieces and create two puzzle sets. Write the Bible verse on the pieces as follows:

He/ is /not /here;/ for/ he/ has/ been/ raised./ (Matthew/ 28:/6a)

Scatter the pieces around the room. Divide the class into two teams. **Say: I will use the slide flute to signal when to begin. Then teams work together to find all the pieces of the verse. The first team to find the words and put them together in the correct order wins.** Suggest the teams use their Bibles if they need some help.

Supplies: Reproducible 6C, marker, Bibles

Zillies: slide flute

Sing

Give each student a copy of the words to the song "He's Alive" **(Reproducible 6E)**. Play the song on the **Cassette** and ask the students to follow along as they listen. Play the song again and invite them to sing with you.

Supplies: Reproducible 6E, cassette player

Zillies: Cassette

Jesus is alive!

OLDER ELEMENTARY 3

Life

Choose one or more activities to bring the Bible to life.

Supplies:
white paper, pencils; paints, crayons, markers, glue and glitter

Zillies:
none

Butterfly Feet?

Say: **The sorrow of the Crucifixion was transformed into the joy of Easter. The butterfly is used as a symbol of Easter. Symbols of the Resurrection are taken from nature and remind us of the good news that Christ has risen. The butterfly is a symbol because early in its growth, it is a hard shell called the chrysalis. It appears dead. But in about two weeks the butterfly breaks out of the chrysalis and flies away—no longer a prisoner in its shell. The butterfly reminds us that Jesus was victorious over death. Jesus lives!**

Ask each student to stand on a white sheet of paper. Show the students how to stand with their legs crossed at the ankles, heels touching, and toes pointed slightly outward. Ask another student to draw around that person's feet with a pencil, following the shape of the feet closely. **Say: Your feet in this position look like a butterfly.**

After each students feet are drawn, ask the students to write the words "Jesus Is Alive!" on the butterflies. Encourage them to add color to the butterflies using paints, crayons, markers, or glue and glitter.

Supplies:
none

Zillies:
none

Sign 'n Pray

each the students how to sign "Jesus Is Alive!" Show them the motions as follows:

Pray, thanking God for Jesus, who died to save the whole world. Thank God for the new life that is offered to each person. Thank God that Christ accepts each person's unique abilities. Ask God's blessings on each person in your class.

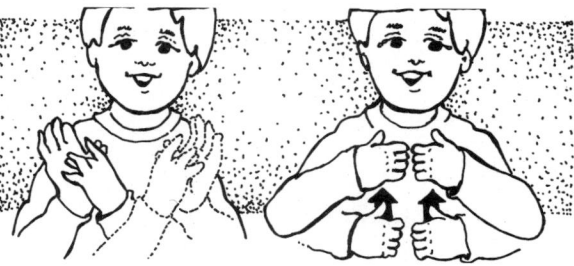

Jesus   Alive

Give each student a copy of HomeZone to enjoy this week.

Home Zone For Students

Butterfly Garden

You can watch caterpillars grow into colorful, lively butterflies. See the caterpillar's transition as it matures, changes into a chrysalid, and finally becomes a painted lady butterfly. A kit is available for you to order. The kit includes a colorful butterfly house, a butterfly feeding kit, instructions on their care, and three to five caterpillars with food. These caterpillars are guaranteed to be perfect specimens. Order from: Insect Lore, P.O. Box 1535, Shafter, CA 93263. You may call toll free 1-800-LIVE-BUG. Ask for the butterfly garden with live caterpillars, #101C, $21.95. (Prices subject to change without notice.)

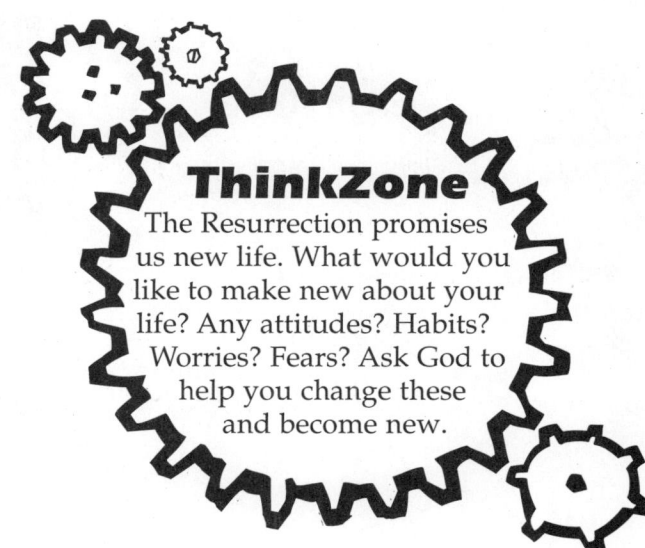

ThinkZone

The Resurrection promises us new life. What would you like to make new about your life? Any attitudes? Habits? Worries? Fears? Ask God to help you change these and become new.

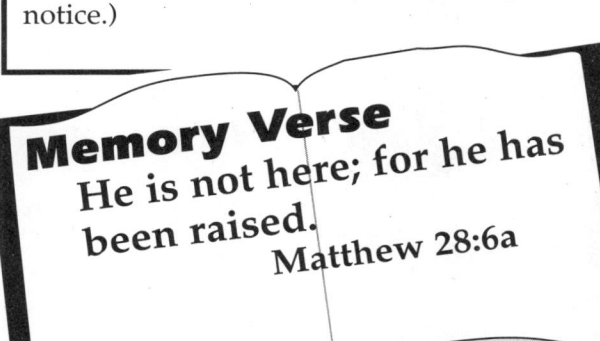

Memory Verse

He is not here; for he has been raised.
— Matthew 28:6a

Hot Cross Buns

Make hot cross buns to share with your family at Easter. You will need:
1 box hot roll mix
⅓ cup sugar
¼ cup seedless raisins
¼ teaspoon allspice
1 teaspoon cinnamon

Prepare the hot roll mix as directed on the package. Add raisins, sugar, cinnamon, and allspice. Divide and shape into buns. Bake as directed on the package.

Make frosting for the buns. You will need:
1 cup confectioner's sugar
2 tablespoons water
2 tablespoons melted butter
Mix together. Add more water if needed to make the frosting spread easily. Spread the frosting over the buns in two lines to form a cross.

Zone In: Jesus is alive!

Reproducible 6D

Permission granted to photocopy for local church use. © 1998 Abingdon Press.

Song

He's Alive

I came to the tomb of Jesus, where once his body lay;
they'd often told me stories that thrilled me day by day.
They told me how he suffered and died on Calvary;
and though I knew that it was true, I wanted now to see

that he's alive and the tomb is empty now!
He rose again by his grand triumphant pow'r.
He's seated now at the Father's own right hand;
the war is won, the work is done and he's alive!

While Jesus walked among us some promises were made;
He told us he'd remember them the way that he had said.
The dead can't keep their promises, and he was crucified;
but all that he has promised me will one day all be mine,

for he's alive and the tomb is empty now!
He rose again by his grand triumphant pow'r.
He's seated now at the Father's own right hand;
the war is won, the work is done and he's alive!
The war is won, the work is done and he's alive!

Words by Herb Owen
© 1989 New Spring Publishing, Inc. (ASCAP), a division of Brentwood-Benson Music Publishing, Inc. All rights reserved. Used by permission.

Walk to Emmaus

Enter the

Bible Verse
Then they told what had happened on the road, and how he (Jesus) had been made known to them in the breaking of the bread.
Luke 24:35

Bible Story
Luke 24:13-35

Just a few hours after the empty tomb had been discovered, two of Jesus' disciples were on their way to the village of Emmaus [i-may'uhs]. The Scriptures do not tell us why they were traveling. Perhaps they were returning to their homes. Perhaps they were leaving Jerusalem to get away from the horror and pain and loss they had experienced there that week.

The road from Jerusalem to Emmaus was only six or seven miles long. As the two disciples walked along, a stranger joined them. He spoke with the disciples, encouraged them, and even explained the Scriptures to them. Even though the disciples had walked and talked with Jesus many times before, they did not recognize him on the road to Emmaus.

It is significant to realize that it was in "the breaking of bread" that these men finally realized that they had been walking and talking with Jesus. At this point they were able to draw on their own experience, to remember the last meal they had shared with Jesus when he also broke bread and blessed it.

The empty tomb had not been enough to convince these followers of Jesus that he had overcome death. It took a personal encounter with him to convince them that Jesus had risen indeed.

On the road to Emmaus the men experienced the presence of Christ. The Resurrection was more than the disappearance of Jesus' body and of the women's discovery of the empty tomb. The risen Lord came to them to reassure them, teach them, and encourage them. Jesus' presence with them gave them the strength and faith to continue his ministry, even though he would no longer be with them in a physical form.

The Emmaus story gives us another important root for our celebration of the Lord's Supper. The Scripture tells us that the disciples knew Jesus "in the breaking of the bread." We recognize Christ when bread is broken in his name—every time.

Jesus Christ is Lord.

Scope the Zone

ZONE	TIME	SUPPLIES	ZILLIES™
Zoom Into the Zone			
Get in the Zone	5 minutes	page 174, cassette player	Cassette
Sandal Slide	15 minutes	Reproducible 7D, waxed paper, tape, large box, scissors	smiley face balloons, slide flute
BibleZone™			
Zoom Into the Bible	15 minutes	Bible for each student, large piece of paper, marker	none
LifeZone			
Detection Perfection	10 minutes	none	slide flute
Bible Scrambler	15 minutes	Bible for each student, Reproducible 7C, scissors, envelopes	none
A Gift So Sweet	10 minutes	Reproducibles 7A, 7B, and 7C	none
Sing	5 minutes	Reproducible 7E, cassette player	Cassette
Remember	15 minutes	plate, bowl of honey: sopaipillas, crackers, or bread	

Zillies™ are found in the **BibleZone™ FUNspirational™ Kit.**

OLDER ELEMENTARY 3

Zoom Into the Zone

Choose one or more activities to catch your children's interest.

Supplies:
page 174, cassette player

Zillies:
Cassette

Get in the Zone

Welcome each student to the BibleZone. **Say: This is the place where we learn God's Word and discover what it means to our lives. This is the place where learning is fun!**

Play "The Bible Zone" **(Cassette)** and invite the students to sing along. Provide copies of the words **(page 174)** for anyone who needs them.

Supplies:
Reproducible 7D, waxed paper, tape, large box, scissors

Zillies:
smiley face balloons, slide flute

Sandal Slide

You will need to play this game in a room or area that is uncarpeted and has a smooth waxed floor. Put a sign that says "Emmaus" on the wall across the room. Under the sign have a large box in which you have placed all of the inflated **smiley face balloons.**

Give each student a copy of the sandal pattern **(Reproducible 7D)** and two large sheets of waxed paper. Have scissors and tape available. Ask the students to use the pattern to make their own sandals out of waxed paper.

Divide the students into two teams (or three teams if you have a large class). Have the teams line up and take off their shoes. Ask them put on their sandals. (This works best if the students wear their socks too.)

Explain: I will use the slide flute to signal the beginning of the relay. A player for each team slides to Emmaus, picks up a smiley face balloon, and slides back to his or her team. The player tags the next player and stands behind the line holding the balloon. When all the balloons in Emmaus are gone, I will use the slide flute to signal to stop. The team holding the most balloons wins. Be careful! If you tear off one of your sandals, you are out of the relay; and if you have a balloon, it goes back to Emmaus.

After the game is over, say: **Something very important happened to two disciples on their walk to Emmaus. We will find out what when we hear the Bible story.**

Jesus Christ is Lord.

BibleZone™

Bible

Choose one or more activities to immerse your children in the Bible story.

Zoom Into the Bible

Be certain each student has a Bible. Divide the class into two teams. Ask Team One to read Luke 24:13-27. Ask Team Two to read Luke 24:28-35.

After the teams have finished reading, talk with the class about the major events of the story. Make a list of the events *(see example)* as they are named. When the list is complete, have the students number off. Then number the list of events, but use descending order (for example, from 14 to 1). Number the list according to the number of students you have. If you have a longer list than number of students, use the numbers again and have the students act out more than one part each (for example, if you have seven students, number the list from 7 to 1 twice).

Example:
1. Two disciples are walking down the road.
2. A stranger joins them, and they do not recognize the stranger.
3. The stranger asks what they are talking about.
4. The disciples ask if the stranger is the only one who does not know the things that have happened in Jerusalem.
5. The stranger asks, "What things?"
6. The disciples tell the stranger about Jesus, the mighty prophet.
7. The disciples tell the stranger about Jesus being handed over, condemned to death, and crucified.
8. The disciples tell the stranger about the women discovering the empty tomb.
9. The stranger teaches the disciples about the Scriptures.
10. The disciples ask the stranger to stay with them because it is getting too late in the day to travel.
11. While sitting at the table, the stranger takes the bread, blesses it, and breaks it.
12. The disciples recognize Jesus.
13. Jesus vanishes from their sight.
14. Immediately the disciples returns to the other disciples and tells them what has happened.

Say: Let's tell the story silently. According to your number, use motions or expressions to tell the event that is happening. Be creative. You may need to ask others to help you tell your part.

Give the students time to organize their plans and to ask one another for help.

Supplies:
Bible for each student, large piece of paper, marker

Zillies:
none

Older Elementary 3

Bible Story

Maria's Gift

by Michael Williams

Maria could not remember when she first started helping her mother in the kitchen. One of the first things she learned was to make bread. Corn tortillas, flour tortillas, the corn meal wrappings for tamales, and her own favorite, sopaipillas. The breads she helped make almost always were filled with wonderful things to eat: beef, chicken, refried beans, chilies, and other tasty treats. Sopaipillas, a fried bread that puffed out to make a pocket into which you could pour honey, was the best of all and was Maria's favorite dessert.

At church she learned about another bread, the bread the priest fed you in the Communion service. As she prepared for her first Communion, she learned that this bread was the body of Christ. She was told that this was the bread of heaven. Father Jose called the bread both of these names.

Maria was so excited as she walked down the aisle in her new white dress. She knelt, and the priest placed the wafer on her tongue. Maria chewed and swallowed. She had never been so disappointed in her life. This didn't taste like bread from heaven. It didn't taste like bread at all. It didn't even taste like food. It tasted like nothing.

Maria walked back down the aisle with her heart in her throat, or maybe that was the lump that the wafer made as she tried to swallow it. She felt sorry for the priests. Was this the kind of bread they had to eat every day? How could they stand it? Perhaps that was why Father Jose looked so sad sometimes. If only he could enjoy some real bread like Mama's tortillas, he would smile. If he could taste her sopaipillas, he would laugh! Maria wondered if Jesus only had that flat, tasteless bread to eat, and she felt sorry for him.

Then Father Joaquin came to help Father Jose. Father Joaquin was young, very young. In fact he looked like a boy not much older than Maria, though she knew he must be in his twenties if he had gone to school to be a priest. He was different in other ways too. He smiled and laughed a lot. While Father Jose was thin and looked as if he never had enough to eat, Father Joaquin appeared to be quite well fed. He had a round face and a round tummy that shook when he laughed hard.

He also told stories about Jesus and his friends. The young priest told them as if they were happening right then and made Maria feel as if she had been there. One day she asked her mother if they could make some sopaipillas for Father Jose and Father Joaquin. Her mother told her that she would be glad to help with such a fine idea. So the two of them made sopaipillas for their two priests.

Maria took the fresh breads to the house by the church where the priests lived. The housekeeper thanked her and closed the door. Once again Maria was disappointed, since she hoped she would see Father Joaquin.

Reproducible 7A

Permission granted to photocopy for local church use. © 1998 Abingdon Press.

The next day Father Joaquin came up to her and told her how good the sopaipillas had been. Then he asked her if she and her mother would be willing to make a few more for Sunday. He had an idea for using them in his sermon. Sopaipillas in a sermon! Maria had never thought of such a thing, but she told him they would be happy to make as many sopaipillas as he needed. He assured her that a few would do.

That next Sunday morning, before the mist had lifted above the nearby mountains, Maria arrived at the church with her basket of warm sopaipillas.

This time she took them directly to the young priest in the church, not the housekeeper. He thanked her and told her to be sure and listen carefully, because he was going to say something very important about her and her delicious baked goods. Maria didn't always listen carefully in church because sometimes it wasn't very interesting to her. But today she knew she would not let a single word slip past her.

When the time for the sermon came in the worship service, Father Joaquin stepped out from behind the pulpit. Maria noticed that he was carrying her basket of sopaipillas.

"This week Maria brought Jesus to me," he began, then fell silent for a long moment. "Then this morning she brought him to me again."

By this time a few of the other children were giggling and looking at Maria. She felt her face getting warm as she wondered what in the world the priest could be talking about.

"Let me tell you a story," he began again, "about a Sunday long ago. Two of Jesus' friends were walking along the road from Jerusalem to Emmaus, which was about seven miles away. A stranger joined them and listened to them talking. They had no idea who the stranger was. He asked them why they were walking along and talking and looking so sad. One of the two friends of Jesus, who was named Cleopas, asked him, 'Are you the only person in Jerusalem who doesn't know what has happened in the past few days?'

"The stranger looked puzzled and asked, 'What are you talking about?' So they told the stranger about Jesus, who had come from Nazareth. They told him how Jesus was a prophet and, like the prophets of old, had gotten into trouble with the religious authorities. The authorities had taken Jesus to the Romans, and Pontius Pilate gave the order to crucify him. Roman soldiers had nailed him to a cross and he had died the death of a criminal, even though he was the Chosen One of God. Then they explained that some women of their group came telling them that they had been to the tomb into which they had seen Jesus placed just before the Sabbath. When they arrived at the tomb this morning, his body was not there.

"They talked until they arrived at Emmaus, and the two asked the stranger to stay and eat with them. Since the road was dark and it wasn't safe to travel alone, he accepted their hospitality.

"As they ate their meal that night, the stranger did the strangest thing. He took a sopaipilla and tore it in half, put honey in each half, and gave it to his two friends who had welcomed him so kindly.

Bible Story

There was something about the way the stranger broke the bread that reminded them of Jesus. Then when they tasted the honey, they were reminded of the sweetness of Jesus' presence; and they recognized the stranger for whom he had been all along. It was Jesus who accompanied them! 'They knew him in the breaking of the bread,' the Scripture tells us.

"Now, every time you break a sopaipilla in half, it can remind you that Jesus accompanies each of you also, even though we don't often recognize him. And the sweetness of the honey will remind you of the sweetness of God's love for each of you children."

Then Father Joaquin broke the sopaipillas Maria had brought him, poured honey in each piece, and gave one to each child. Though she had been told as she prepared for her first Communion that the priest represented Christ, she had never understood that until now. This round, gentle man who laughed easily and told stories made her think of Jesus in a way no one had before or since.

It was years later that Maria realized that Father Joaquin had added the part about sopaipilla and honey. In the Bible the stranger just breaks the bread and they recognize who the stranger is—Jesus. While Maria's teachers had taught her that the Bible was correct, she continued to imagine a smiling, round-faced Jesus feeding those he loved the bread and honey that the young priest had shared after the story.

For the rest of her life every time she tore a sopaipilla and filled the halves with honey, Maria felt as if Jesus sat right there with her, reminding her of the sweetness of God's love.

Then	they	told	what	had	happened
on	the	road	and	how	he
(Jesus)	had	been	made	known	to
them	in	the	breaking	of	the
bread.	Luke	24:	35		

Reproducible 7C

Permission granted to photocopy for local church use. © 1998 Abingdon Press.

Choose one or more activities to bring the Bible to life.

Detection Perfection

Supplies: none

Zillies: slide flute

Divide the students into two teams. Have the teams stand in a line facing one another. **Say: Sometimes we think we see everything, but often we don't. Let's play a game to see how well you can detect. You will be playing against the person standing in front of you.**

Name the teams the Detectives and the Suspects. **Explain: The Detectives will be given one minute to look carefully at the Suspects. Then the Detectives will turn their backs to the Suspects and cover their eyes with their hands. Each of the Suspects will do something to change his or her appearance: remove jewelry, untuck a shirt, take off glasses.** (Do not give too many suggestions so that the students will be inventive.) **Then the Detectives will uncover their eyes and look again at the Suspects to see if they detect any changes. You will have one minute to detect changes. I will be using the slide flute to signal times.**

Play again, this time reversing which team is the Detectives and which team is the Suspects. Keep score and repeat play several times.

Say: Jesus' disciples did not recognize him after the Resurrection. What did Jesus do that helped the disciples to know him? *(blessed the bread and broke it)*

Bible Scrambler

Supplies: Bible for each student, Reproducible 7C, scissors, envelopes

Zillies: none

Photocopy and cut apart several copies of the Bible verse cards (**bottom half, Reproducible 7C**) so that you have a set for every three or four students. Place each scrambled set in a separate envelope. Place the envelopes in different areas of the room where the students will be able to spread them out.

Ask the students to read today's Bible verse with you one time: "Then they told what had happened on the road, and how he (Jesus) had been made known to them in the breaking of the bread" (Luke 24:35). Then ask everyone to close his or her Bibles.

Divide the students into teams of three or four. **Say: There are envelopes placed around the room that contain today's Bible verse. Work with your team members to get the verse put in the correct order. Let's see which team finishes first.**

OLDER ELEMENTARY 3

Life

Choose one or more activities to bring the Bible to life.

Supplies:
Reproducible 7A, 7B, and 7C

Zillies:
none

A Gift So Sweet

Read or tell the story "Maria's Gift" **(Reproducible 7A, 7B, and 7C).** Ask: Do you enjoy any kind of sweets? What are some of the sweetest experiences of your life? In the story, whenever Maria hears the word bread, she thinks of the bread her mother makes. What is your favorite kind of bread? Why? When you go up for Communion, does the bread remind you of any experience you have had in your daily life?

Say: Every time we eat bread, we can think of Jesus, not just at Communion. For example, if you have toast for breakfast, while you eat you can think of Jesus and the sweetness of God's love.

Supplies:
Reproducible 7E, cassette player

Zillies:
Cassette

Sing

Give each student a copy of the words to the song "He Is Lord" **(Reproducible 7E).** Play the song on the **Cassette** and ask the students to follow along. Play the song again and invite them to sing.

Say: The disciples learned that Jesus is Lord. Jesus died and was buried. Jesus rose from the dead and returned to his disciples. He walked with them, talked with them, taught them, ate with them. He blessed the bread and broke it so they would remember him. Jesus helped the disciples become strong. They discovered without a doubt that Jesus is Lord.

Supplies:
plate, bowl of honey; sopaipillas, crackers, or bread

Zillies:
none

Remember

Place a small bowl of honey in the center of a plate. Place torn sopaipillas, crackers, or pieces of bread around the honey. Ask the students to join you in a circle. Invite each student to take a sopaipilla, cracker, or bread and dip it in the honey. Before eating, **pray**: Dear God, we thank you for your Son, Jesus. We ask that as we eat this food, we remember Jesus. Help each us to know Jesus Christ personally as our Lord and Savior. Amen.

Give each student a copy of HomeZone to enjoy this week.

BIBLEZONE™

Home Zone For Students

Bread Bonanza

The disciples remembered Jesus when he blessed the bread and broke it. Each time we have Communion, we remember Jesus.

You can make "permanent" bread, a sculpture, to keep as a remembrance of Jesus. You will need:
a large bowl and spoon
4 cups of sawdust
1 cup of wheat paste
2½ cups of water

Combine all the ingredients with a large spoon. Knead the dough with your hands.

Put the dough on a piece of aluminum foil or waxed paper. Form the dough into the shape of a loaf of bread. Let your sculpture dry and harden. When it is completely dry, you can paint the sculpture if you want to or spray it with clear enamel to make it shiny.

Use your sculpture as a centerpiece on your table at home.

ThinkZone

Is Jesus Lord of your life? How can you show your friends that Jesus is Lord?

Sopaipillas

You can make sopaipillas to enjoy with your family. You will need to ask an adult to help you fry the sopaipillas. You will need:
¾ cups flour
2 teaspoons baking powder
1 teaspoon salt
2 tablespoons shortening
⅔ cup cold water
oil for frying

Sift flour, baking powder, and salt into bowl. Cut in shortening until crumbly. Add enough cold water gradually to form dough. Knead gently on a lightly floured surface until the dough is smooth. Cover the dough and let it "rest" for five minutes. Roll the dough into a 12 x 15-inch rectangle ⅛-inch thick. Cut into 3x3 or 2x3-inch pieces. Preheat oil in a saucepan to 400 degrees. Drop a few pieces at a time into the oil. Fry them to two to three minutes on each side or until puffed, turning several times to brown evenly. Serve your sopaipillas with honey.

Memory Verse

Then they told what had happened on the road, and how he (Jesus) had been made known to them in the breaking of the bread. Luke 24:35

Zone IN: Jesus Christ is Lord.

Permission granted to photocopy for local church use. © 1998 Abingdon Press.

Older Elementary 3

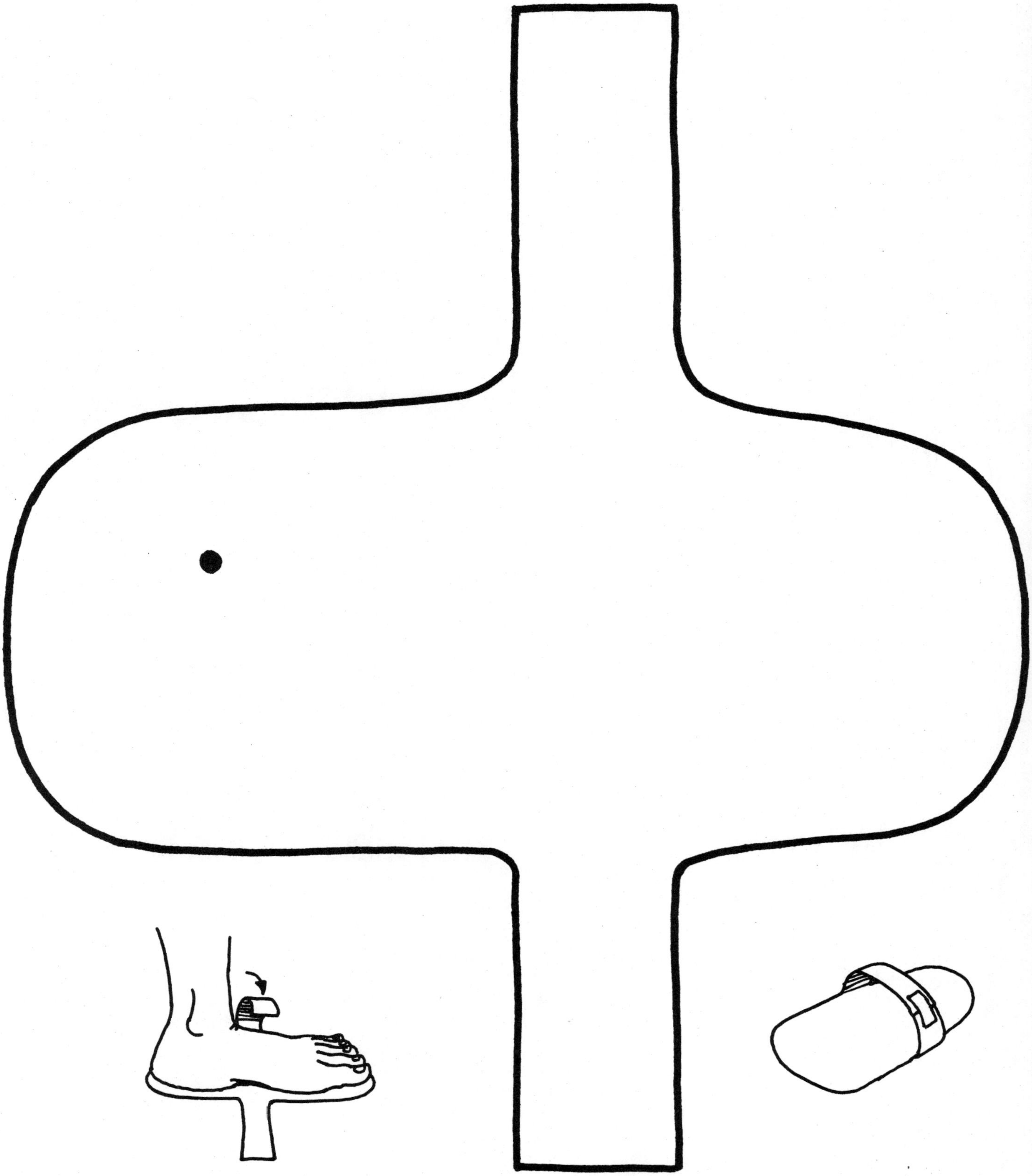

Reproducible 7D

Song

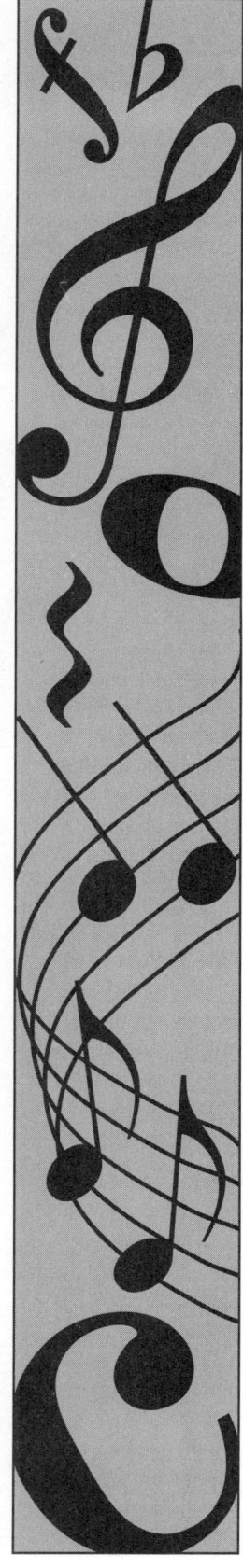

He Is Lord

He is Lord, he is Lord.
He is risen from the dead and he is Lord.
Every knee shall bow, every tongue confess
That Jesus Christ is Lord.

He is Lord, he is Lord.
He is risen from the dead and he is Lord.
Every knee shall bow, every tongue confess
That Jesus Christ is Lord.

He is Lord, he is Lord.
He is risen from the dead and he is Lord.
Every knee shall bow, every tongue confess
That Jesus Christ is Lord.

Jesus Christ is Lord.

Arr. © 1996 New Spring Publishing, Inc. (ASCAP), admin. by Brentwood-Benson Music Publishing, Inc. All rights reserved. Used by permission.

8 Bible

Jesus and the Fishermen

Enter the

Bible Verse
Jesus said, "Follow me, and I will make you fish for people."

Matthew 4:19b, adapted

Bible Story
Matthew 4:18-22; Mark 1:16-20; Luke 5:1-11

Early in his ministry Jesus gathered disciples around him. Out of the many who followed him, Jesus chose twelve to be with him. Lists of the twelve are found in Mark 3:13-19, Matthew 10:1-4, and Luke 6:12-16.

Luke 5:1-11 describes Jesus' performing a symbolic miracle before calling Peter, James, and John to be his disciples. They had fished all night and had caught nothing. When Jesus told Simon Peter to put his nets into the water, Simon's nets were filled with so many fish that he needed help to get them to shore. Jesus told them that from that moment on, their work would be catching people rather than fish.

All four Gospel accounts tell us that the response to Jesus' call was immediate and without question. Luke says, "They left everything and followed him." Matthew and Mark are almost identical in their accounts. Jesus called to Simon and Andrew, and immediately they left their means of livelihood and followed Jesus. Jesus called James and John, and they too responded immediately.

Andrew was the brother of Simon Peter and the son of Jonas, or John of Bethsaida, in Galilee. Andrew was one of Jesus' twelve disciples and, according to the Gospel of John, the person who introduced Simon to Jesus. Although Andrew appeared to have a quieter nature than Peter, he emerged as a leader among the twelve disciples. Andrew brought the boy with the loaves and fishes to Jesus. He was a devoutly religious disciple who thoughtfully influenced others.

There were three disciples in the "inner circle": Simon, whom Jesus later called Peter; and the two sons of Zebedee, James and John. In the Gospels these three are often singled out, and they became prominent leaders of the Christian movement after Jesus' death and resurrection. Peter became recognized after Jesus' death as the foremost apostle.

We can be disciples of Jesus.

Scope the Zone

ZONE	TIME	SUPPLIES	ZILLIES™
Zoom Into the Zone			
Get in the Zone	5 minutes	page 174, cassette player	Cassette
Fish Friends	5 minutes	Reproducible 8D, scissors, basket, safety pins or tape	none
Fish Tag	15 minutes	none	inflatable fish, fish erasers, slide flute
BibleZone™			
Zoom Into the Bible	20 minutes	Bible for each student, Reproducible 8C, pencils, slips of paper	slide flute
Funny Fish	15 minutes	Reproducible 8D, crayons or markers	none
LifeZone			
Bulls-Eye!	15 minutes	Reproducible 8C, large piece of paper, marker, tape	sponge ball, slide flute
Fish Flop	10 minutes	Bible for each student	inflatable fish
Sing	5 minutes	Reproducible 8E, cassette player	Cassette
Gone Fishin'	10 minutes	Reproducibles 8A and 8B	none
Go Fish	15 minutes	slips of paper, paper clips or safety pins, pens or pencils	net square

Zillies™ are found in the **BibleZone™ FUNspirational™ Kit.**

OLDER ELEMENTARY 3

Zoom Into the Zone

Choose one or more activities to catch your children's interest.

Supplies:
page 174,
cassette player

Zillies:
Cassette

Get in the Zone

Greet each student enthusiastically. Have "The Bible Zone" playing on the **Cassette** as they enter the room. Invite them to sing with you. Have copies of the words available **(page 174)** for anyone who needs them.

Say: The Bible is so incredible! The Bible is the Word of God! The stories in the Bible tell us of the power and love of God and of God's Son, Jesus.

Supplies:
Reproducible 8D,
scissors, basket,
safety pins or tape

Zillies:
none

Fish Friends

Make enough copies of the fish cards **(Reproducible 8D)** that you will have one card per student. Cut out the cards and put them in a basket face down. Ask the students to take one card from the basket and to tape or pin it on their clothing.

Say: Look at everyone's fish card. Find the person who is wearing a fish card just like yours. That person will be your "fish friend," your disciple partner today. (You may need to wear a card in order to have pairs if you have an uneven number of students.)

Supplies:
none

Zillies:
inflatable fish,
fish erasers,
slide flute

Fish Tag

Think of a creative way to determine which pair of disciple partners will be "It" for this game. For example, toss the **inflatable fish** in the air. Ask the students to try to catch it. The student who catches the fish becomes "It" along with that student's disciple partner.

Give all the students except the ones who are "It" a **fish eraser**. Say: Put the eraser on your head. You must keep the eraser on your head and keep from being tagged. If you are tagged or if the eraser falls off your head, you and your disciple partner automatically become "It." Use the **slide flute** to signal when to begin play.

We can be disciples of Jesus.

BibleZone™

Bible

Choose one or more activities to immerse your children in the Bible story.

Zoom Into the Bible

Say: A disciple is a learner or a student, a person who chooses to follow a teacher or a teaching. Disciple is the word we use to describe Jesus' twelve closest friends, but also people who have chosen to follow Jesus since that time. The Bible lists the names of the first twelve disciples.

Be sure each student has a Bible. Ask the disciple partners to sit together. Give each pair a copy of "Disguised Disciples" **(top half, Reproducible 8C)**. Say: Work with your disciple partner to unscramble the names of the first twelve disciples. I will give you four minutes. I will use the slide flute to tell you when to stop. You may begin now.

After four minutes signal the students with the **slide flute**. Say: **How many partners unscrambled all of the names? If you need help, look in your Bibles at Matthew 10:1-4.** *(1. Peter; 2. James; 3. Bartholomew; 4. John; 5. Thomas; 6. Judas; 7. Andrew; 8. Thaddaeus; 9. Matthew; 10. Philip; 11. Simon; 12. James)*

Prepare slips of paper that have a 1, 2, or 3 on them. Put them in a basket face down. Ask each pair of the disciple partners to pick one. Ask them to read the following Scriptures according to which number they drew from the basket. Number 1 reads Matthew 4:18-22. Number 2 reads Mark 1:16-20. Number 3 reads Luke 5:1-11.

Talk about the Scriptures. **Ask: How did the fishermen respond to Jesus?** *(They left everything and followed him immediately.)* **What did Jesus tell the fishermen they would do?** *(fish for people)*

Supplies:
Bible for each student, Reproducible 8C, pencils, slips of paper

Zillies:
slide flute

Funny Fish

Say: The fish is an important symbol for Christians. It reminds us of the fishermen that Jesus called to be his disciples.

Give each student a copy of the fish cards **(Reproducible 8D)**. Say: **These fish are doing things we do every day. What if Jesus came to you while you were blowing bubbles or working out or reading a book, what would you think? What would you have to do to follow Jesus and fish for people?** Invite the students to color the pictures while they talk.

Supplies:
Reproducible 8D, crayons or markers

Zillies:
none

OLDER ELEMENTARY 3

Bible Zone Story

Fishing for Christmas
by Michael Williams

"Where are the presents?" everyone asked when Meemaw arrived. Meemaw was the special name by which all the grandchildren knew their mother's mother. Usually she arrived with the old station wagon loaded with carefully wrapped presents for each person in the family. Until this year she had arrived with Papa too.

Their mother's father, Papa, had died suddenly of a heart attack last March. There hadn't been time to write any last letters or even make a last phone call. One minute he was there and the next he was gone. Even Meemaw didn't have time to say good-bye to him. This would be their first Christmas without Papa.

But where were the presents? "This year will be different. I have a big surprise on Christmas. I'm going to take you where Papa always wanted to take you for Christmas. Just be ready to spend a few hours with me on Christmas Day. And don't ask too many questions," Meemaw said.

It was easy for Mom and Dad not to ask too many questions. But Jimmy and I were just kids. It was our job to ask too many questions. It was also our job to open the presents, if any presents ever showed up.

My name is Joanna, but everybody calls me Johnny. I'm twelve and Jimmy is ten. We are pretty close as far as brothers and sisters go. I'm big for my age and I am good at sports. So Jimmy helps me with my homework and piano lessons, and I help him with his soccer and softball. Not a bad arrangement.

Well, Christmas morning dawned and still no presents from Meemaw. By this time Jimmy and I had decided that Papa's death had gotten to her, and she was getting a little strange. After all of the other presents had been opened and the paper and ribbons were scattered from one end of the den to the other, Meemaw finally said, "Well, I guess it's time for your surprise."

She asked Jimmy and me to go with her to the station wagon. When we got there, she took out a package wrapped in brown paper. Could this be the big surprise? We helped her bring it inside; but before she would let us unwrap it, she announced, "I'm taking you fishing for Christmas."

"Fishing!" we all exclaimed at once. Meemaw had never been fishing in her life, not that we knew about, anyway.

"Isn't it too cold to go fishing?" I asked, forgetting the warning about too many questions. I guess Meemaw had forgotten too.

"It's never too cold to go fishing," she answered, "and here is your equipment."

Jimmy and I tore into the package like a couple of buzz saws. When we got them open, though, there were no fishing poles or tackle. Much to our surprise there were five aprons, all alike but different sizes. They were all bright red and had "God is love" written across the bib part. Under these were a bunch of those padded gloves that people use when they take hot dishes out of the oven or when they grill out.

Reproducible 8A

"When do we leave?" asked Jimmy. As if we really could go fishing in aprons and padded gloves.

"Not for a while," Meemaw told him. "I'll let you know when the time is right."

We all had our traditional Christmas breakfast, where everybody ate too much and then complained about feeling too full. Then we just sort of laid around waiting for the next crazy thing to happen. About 10:30 that morning Meemaw started gathering her things.

"Get your aprons and mitts," she called out. "We can't fish without aprons and mitts." When we got out into the driveway, she added, "I'll drive."

We all climbed into the old station wagon and stared at Meemaw as she drove. I guess we all just had to be sure she hadn't gone completely off her rocker.

We hadn't gone very far before Mom said, "Mother, you realize that you're driving us downtown?"

"That's right, Dear," was all Meemaw said.

When we got downtown, we stopped in front of an old brick church building in a rundown neighborhood.

"Okay, let's go fishing." Meemaw led the way into the building. A white-haired man wearing a different apron greeted her. She told him our names and said, "We're here to serve."

Well, for the next two hours my family stood behind a hot table like the one in the school cafeteria and served Christmas dinner to people who didn't have any homes and wouldn't have had any dinner except for us and the other volunteers. Meemaw greeted everyone who ate with a cheerful, "Merry Christmas."

I still didn't see where any of this had anything to do with fishing. So on the way home, I asked Meemaw, "When do we get to the fishing part?"

"Oh, we've already done the fishing part," she said. "Your grandfather always wanted to do something like this for Christmas. I was the one who wanted it to be a holiday at home with just our family. Then after he died, I started reading his Bible. I noticed he had underlined many parts of it. One day I happened upon the part where Jesus is calling disciples who fish for a living. He tells them that if they follow him, he will teach them how to fish for people. Out in the margin your grandfather had written, 'Goin' fishin' some Christmas soon.' I realized that he saw feeding the hungry as the kind of fishing Jesus was talking about. Just telling people who don't feel loved that God is love is another way of feeding them. That's when I decided we would go fishing this Christmas. That's when I decided that this Christmas I would give you all the present he had wanted to give you for so long."

"You don't have to come with me, but every year, as long as I'm able, I intend to be at that very same place, wearing my 'God is love' apron and fishing the way Jesus taught us to. You don't have to go with me if you don't want to."

"We probably will," Jimmy spoke up, "now that we know you're not off your rocker." Our laughter filled the station wagon like the spirit of Christmas.

Disguised Disciples

1. eterp _____
2. asemj _____
3. ooeawmlhrtb _____
4. njho _____
5. shmtoa _____
6. uasdj _____
7. wdnrea _____
8. dathseuda _____
9. taewhtm _____
10. iilpph _____
11. iomns _____
12. jsmea _____

D I S C I
P L E S

Reproducible 8C
Permission granted to photocopy for local church use. © 1998 Abingdon Press.

Life

Choose one or more activities to bring the Bible to life.

Bulls-Eye!

Have two pairs of "disciples" play this game at a time or make enough copies that several pairs could play at the same time. Cut apart the bulls-eye letters **(bottom half, Reproducible 8C)** and tape them to a wall, door, or table turned on its side. Spread them out so there is some space between each letter.

Say: A disciple is a person who learns and then shares what he or she has learned with other people. In this game we will think about the characteristics of a disciple; for example, what sort of person he or she should be, how a disciple should act, what a disciple should say.

Give each pair six of the **sponge balls. Say: I will use the slide flute to signal when to begin. One person from each pair is to throw a sponge ball at the letters. Whichever letter is hit with the ball is the one your pair must play. What word that begins with that letter describes a disciple? You cannot use a word that has already been used. If you cannot think of a word, say "pass."**

Write the words and keep score for the pairs. When all of the sponge balls have been thrown, begin play with new pairs of disciples.

Supplies:
Reproducible 8C, large piece of paper, marker, tape

Zillies:
sponge balls, slide flute

Fish Flop

Ask the students to find today's Bible verse in their Bibles and read it with you: "Jesus said, 'Follow me, and I will make you fish for people'" (Matthew 4:19b, adapted).

Say: Close your Bibles. We will see how well we can remember the verse.

Ask everyone to stand in a circle. Toss the **inflatable fish** in the air. **Say: Anyone who lets the fish flop on the floor has to say the Bible verse.** Continue play until you are certain everyone knows the Bible verse.

Supplies:
Bible for each student

Zillies:
inflatable fish

We can be disciples of Jesus.

OLDER ELEMENTARY 3

Life

Choose one or more activities to bring the Bible to life.

Supplies:
Reproducible 8E, cassette player

Zillies:
Cassette

Sing

Give each student a copy of the words to the song "I Have Decided to Follow Jesus" **(Reproducible 8E)**. Play the song on the **Cassette** and ask the students to follow along as they listen. Play the song again and invite them to sing.

Ask: What do you think Jesus meant when he said, "I will make you fish for people"? *(The disciples were to help others learn about Jesus.)* **What are some ways we can fish for people today?** *(by inviting others to Sunday school, by behaving so that others will see God's love in our lives)*

Supplies:
Reproducibles 8A and 8B

Zillies:
none

Gone Fishin'

Read or tell the story "Fishing for Christmas" **(Reproducibles 8A and 8B)**. Ask: **What were some ways Johnny and Jimmy became fishermen? What did they do that made them disciples who follow Jesus?**

Supplies:
slips of paper, paper clips or safety pins, pens or pencils

Zillies:
net square

Go Fish

"Follow   me."

Teach the students how to sign the words "Follow Me."

Hang the **net square** on the wall. Give each student a slip of paper and a pencil. **Say: Today we talked about being disciples. We can be disciples of Jesus. Write on the paper one thing you will do this week that shows you are a disciple of Jesus.** Ask each of the disciple partners to go to the fish net. **Say: One of you may sign to your partner "Follow me" while the other pins his or her paper on the fish net. Then reverse.**

Give time for each pair of partners to go to the fish net. **Pray: Dear God, when Jesus calls us, we will fish for people. We will be kind and thoughtful. We will help others and tell them about Jesus and about your love. Amen.**

Give each student a copy of HomeZone to enjoy this week.

Home Zone For Students

A Secret Sign

The fish has been a symbol of discipleship since the time of the first disciples. The Greek word for fish is *ikhthus* (IK thus). These letters represent the first letters of the Greek words for Jesus Christ, Son of God.

In the early history of the church, Christians were persecuted and often killed. The symbol of the fish was used as a secret code to identify other Christians. When talking with a stranger, the Christian would draw the symbol of the fish in the dirt with his or her foot. If the stranger saw the fish and then drew a fish with his or her foot, both people would know the other was a Christian. If the stranger was not a Christian, the fish would mean nothing to him. The Christian's religious beliefs remained a secret and he or she was safe.

Sandpaint a fish symbol to keep in your room. Lightly brush glue over a small piece of cardboard. Sprinkle uncolored sand over the glue. Let it dry and gently shake off the excess. Add powdered tempera paint to sand to create colored sand. Use glue to outline a fish symbol on top of the sand. Sprinkle the colored sand on top of the glue outline. Let it dry and gently shake off the excess.

ThinkZone
Jesus said, "Follow me." Do you have friends or relatives who do not follow Jesus? Is there a way that you can be a disciple and tell them about Jesus?

Memory Verse
Jesus said, "Follow me, and I will make you fish for people."
Matthew 4:19b, adapted

Fishbait Cups

- 2 cups cold milk
- 1 package chocolate instant pudding mix
- gummy worms
- 1 8-ounce tub of Cool Whip topping, thawed
- 1 16-ounce package of chocolate cookies, crushed
- 8 to 10 (7-ounce) plastic cups

Mix the instant pudding and milk according to directions on the package. Stir in the Cool Whip topping and half of the crushed cookies. Put 1 tablespoon of crushed cookies in the bottom of each cup. Add pudding mixture so that the cups are ¾ full. Top with the remaining crushed cookies. Refrigerate one hour. Poke gummy worms down into the cups so that they appear to be sticking out of the dirt!

We can be disciples of Jesus.

Reproducible 8D

Permission granted to photocopy for local church use. © 1998 Abingdon Press.

Song

I Have Decided to Follow Jesus

I have decided to follow Jesus;
I have decided to follow Jesus;
I have decided to follow Jesus;
No turning back, no turning back.

Tho' none will join me, still I will follow;
Tho' none will join me, still I will follow;
Tho' none will join me, still I will follow;
No turning back, no turning back.

The world behind me, the cross before me;
The world behind me, the cross before me;
The world behind me, the cross before me;
No turning back, no turning back.

No turning back, no
No turning back, now, no turning back now.

I have decided to follow Jesus;
I have decided to follow Jesus;
I have decided to follow Jesus;
No turning back, no turning back.

I have decided to follow Jesus;
I have decided to follow Jesus;
I have decided to follow Jesus;
No turning back, no turning back.

Arr. © 1995 Bridge Building Music, Inc. (BMI), admin. by Brentwood-Benson Music Publishing, Inc. All Rights Reserved. Used by permission.

9 BibleZone

Jesus and Levi

Enter the Zone

Bible Verse
Jesus said to him, "Follow me." And he got up, left everything, and followed him.

Luke 5:27b, 28, adapted

Bible Story
Mark 2:13-1; Luke 5:27-32

A question that interests many Bible scholars is whether or not Matthew the disciple and Levi the tax collector are the same person. Matthew is listed in the Gospels of Matthew, Mark, and Luke as one of the twelve disciples. According to the Gospel of Matthew he was a tax collector who was sitting in his toll booth when Jesus passed by and called him (Matthew 9:9). Later this Gospel lists the same man as one of the disciples (10:3). Mark and Luke also include the story of the tax collector, but they name him Levi and do not identify him with the disciple Matthew.

Tax collectors were regarded by other Jews as contemptible and corrupt. They were considered collaborators with the Roman rulers. Tax collectors often extorted more taxes than were required by the government and kept the excess money.

Jesus called the first twelve disciples from a variety of occupations and backgrounds. Jesus did not select them based on their religious ideas or status in life. Jesus chose ordinary people to learn from him and to preach his teachings.

Jesus went to dinner at Levi's home. The religious leaders questioned why Jesus would eat with people who were considered no different than sinners and criminals. Jesus answered their questions by reminding them that the well did not need a physician.

Jesus called a man who was a social outcast to follow him. Levi left his despised but profitable occupation to follow Jesus.

Every person can be a follower of Jesus.

Scope the Zone

ZONE	TIME	SUPPLIES	ZILLIES™
Zoom Into the Zone			
Get in the Zone	5 minutes	page 174, cassette player	Cassette
Mad Tax	15 minutes	Reproducible 9C, crayons, markers, scissors, tape	gold coins
BibleZone™			
Zoom Into the Bible	15 minutes	Bible for each student	none
Play in a Bag	15 minutes	two large bags, paper plates, cups, yarn, two pieces of paper, two pairs of tennis shoes	gold coins, fish erasers, shoelaces
LifeZone			
Followers' Folly	10 minutes	none	hose
Levi's Lesson	10 minutes	Reproducibles 9A and 9B	none
Sing	5 minutes	Reproducible 9E, cassette player	Cassette
Money Rub	15 minutes	Reproducible 9D, pencils, tape, crayons, gold pencils or pens	gold coins
Sign 'n Pray	5 minutes	none	none

Zillies™ are found in the **BibleZone™ FUNspirational™ Kit.**

OLDER ELEMENTARY 3

Zoom Into the Zone

Choose one or more activities to catch your children's interest.

Supplies:
page 174,
cassette player

Zillies:
Cassette

Get in the Zone

Welcome each student enthusiastically. Have "The Bible Zone" playing on the **Cassette** as the students enter the room. Have copies of the words **(page 174)** available if anyone needs them.

Supplies:
Reproducible 9C;
crayons, markers;
scissors, tape

Zillies:
gold coins

Mad Tax

Give each student a copy of the tax collector's hat **(Reproducible 9C)**. Invite the students to decorate the hats, cut them out, and tape the strips to the hat to make them fit around their heads.

Ask the students to number off. **Say: Students with even numbers, put your hats down for a while. You will be citizens. Students with even numbers, put your hats on. You will be tax collectors.**

Give each student an equal number of **gold coins. Say: The tax collectors are out to get your money. There is no telling how much they will get from you.**

Explain how to play: Each of the tax collectors go to the citizens. Both of you hold out some of your gold coins, but not all of them. It's up to you how many you hold out. Tax collector, you say odd or even. Then both of you count how many coins you have. If you have an even number of coins and the tax collector said even, the tax collector keeps all of the coins you both held out. If there is an odd number of coins and the tax collector said even, then the citizen gets to keep all the coins you both held out.

Tax collectors must go around the room and tax all of the citizens. After everyone has been taxed, the tax collector with the most money wins.

Have the students swap roles. Have the citizens put on their tax collector hats and become the collectors. Begin the game again with everyone having an equal number of coins.

Say: Our Bible story today is about a tax collector. People often hated tax collectors because they were unfair. But today we will find out how the life of one tax collector was changed.

BibleZone™

Bible Zone

Choose one or more activities to immerse your children in the Bible story.

Zoom Into the Bible

Be certain each student has a Bible. Divide the students into two teams. Ask Team One to read Mark 2:13-17. Ask Team Two to read Luke 5:27-32.

Ask the following questions:
1. Who was Levi? *(a tax collector)*
2. What did Jesus say to Levi? *(Follow me.)*
3. What did Levi do? *(left everything and followed Jesus)*
4. Where was the dinner held that night? *(at Levi's house)*
5. What did the Pharisees ask Jesus? *(Why do you eat with tax collectors and sinners?)*
6. What did Jesus answer? *(Those who are well have no need of a physician.)*

Supplies:
Bible for each student

Zillies:
none

Play in a Bag

Ask the students to remain with their teams. Give each team a large paper bag. Have the following items in each bag: paper plates, cups, yarn, a piece of paper, **gold coins, fish erasers, shoelaces,** and a pair of tennis shoes.

Say: Now each team will become the cast of a play. Each team has a bag of props to use. Tell today's Bible story using the props and body language only, no words.

Have the teams take turns presenting their plays. Have one team be the audience while the other team performs. To make the experience more challenging for the actors and the audience, have the actors present the events of the story out of order and have the audience guess what is happening.

Supplies:
two large bags,
paper plates,
cups, yarn,
two pieces of paper,
two pairs of tennis shoes

Zillies:
gold coins,
fish erasers,
shoelaces

> **Every person can be a follower of Jesus.**

OLDER ELEMENTARY 3

Bible Zone Story

Levi, The Tax Guy
by Michael Williams

Levi had been working for the Internal Revenue Service since he graduated from college. He had married his high school sweetheart, Marilyn, and in time they became the parents of Harry and Georgia. Levi went on to earn his masters degree in business administration by attending classes at night at a local university. He had everything that any person could want. He had a great family, and they lived in a nice neighborhood in a modest house. They even had a dog and two cars. He and Marilyn both served in leadership roles in their church, and the children were active in the children's ministry and youth group. Levi was living the American dream.

There was just one problem: Levi wasn't satisfied. The more he achieved, the more he realized he had not achieved. He still worked in the same department in which he had begun fifteen years ago. He had been promoted through the ranks until now he was head of the department. He was a good leader, and his co-workers respected him. He liked his work and felt that he was making a contribution. He had always been good at math and liked to see things add up. Still, for all the good things in his life, something didn't add up; and he just couldn't put his finger on what was missing.

Levi knew that many people hated the Internal Revenue Service. No one liked to pay taxes, but everyone liked the things for which his or her taxes paid. Levi believed in what he did for a living. He was honest and expected other people to be honest as well. Then all his department would have to do is look for honest mistakes.

Levi did try to keep a sense of humor about his job. His kids made sure he didn't miss the humorous side of things. They called him The Tax Guy. With his and Marilyn's help, Georgia and Harry made a home video entitled "The Attack of the One Hundred Foot Tax Guy." Besides the sound of the title, it was a pretty bad movie with lots of scenes of their dad's foot crashing through the roofs of cardboard houses. It still left the whole family rolling in the floor crying with laughter. The movie became a family joke. You had to be a participant to appreciate its full effect.

Then one Sunday night the kids came home from the church youth group talking about a mission trip to the area along the border between the United States and Mexico. They would need adults to travel and work with them. Harry and Georgia were still young enough to want their father to go along, and they were able to convince Levi that was what he should do. They spent the next nine months raising money with bake sales and car washes and hiring out to work for members of the congregation. They bought and borrowed equipment to take along with donated supplies so they would have what they would need to rebuild a church building during the day and lead a vacation Bible school in the evenings.

After three long days of driving, the team finally arrived. A few of the people had taken high school Spanish classes, but they soon discovered that the people with whom they would work spoke both English and Spanish.

Reproducible 9A

Permission granted to photocopy for local church use. © 1998 Abingdon Press.

Pastor Lopez greeted each of them personally and welcomed them on behalf of the congregation. When Levi introduced himself, the pastor startled him by responding, "Oh, the tax guy."

Levi looked at Harry and Harry looked at Georgia and Georgia looked at her dad. How could Pastor Lopez have known?

Seeing the confusion his remark had created, the pastor quickly added, "You know, Levi in the Bible—who is also called Matthew—was a tax collector who became a disciple. It was a little joke." The three breathed a sigh of relief that their host didn't have ESP.

Levi always had been told that he was named after a great-grandfather. He had never thought about the origin of his name beyond that. But that night before he went to sleep, Levi got out his Bible. (Like everyone else, he had brought a Bible because it was included on the packing list the youth director had given them.) He found that Levi was never directly called Matthew in the Bible, but he appeared on a list of the closest followers of Jesus.

The passing comment by the pastor kept coming to Levi's mind during the daytime as he was sawing and driving nails, and at night while teaching songs to the children of the village. The ancient Levi was a follower of Jesus, who left a job collecting taxes to join the rabbi's group of friends. The modern Levi had been a member of the church all his life, but he had never thought of himself as a follower of Jesus. But now, working with his hands under the south Texas sun and learning to love these children who had so little of the life his own children enjoyed, he felt closer to Jesus then he ever had.

After they returned home, Levi, Georgia, and Harry would offer as a family to speak to church groups about the trip. Levi found that he had a gift for speaking to groups, especially about an experience as important to him as the mission trip had been. That fall Levi enrolled in a long-term Bible study that met once a week throughout the school year. He learned more about the Scriptures Jesus would have read, which he had learned to call the Old Testament. Then he learned more about the stories of Jesus and his friends in the New Testament. The more he learned, the more he wanted to learn. Also, he began to learn Spanish so when he returned to south Texas he could speak to the people in their first language rather than expecting them to speak in his.

After three mission trips and three years of intense Bible study, Levi sat down with Marilyn, Harry, and Georgia for a family meeting. Levi wanted to begin to take courses at a local seminary where people trained for full-time ministry. Did this mean he was going to stop being The Tax Guy? He wasn't sure yet, but since the decision would affect the whole family, he wanted to talk it over with them. Harry would go to college the next year, and Georgia would be a high school junior. It would be very difficult to change careers at this time.

Would Levi become a pastor or a missionary? Would he remain an active member of his congregation and continue to learn and go on mission trips? He did not have the answers to these questions. Only God knew. The one thing Levi did know was that he would never think of himself as anything other than a follower of Jesus.

Reproducible 9C

Permission granted to photocopy for local church use. © 1998 Abingdon Press.

BibleZone™

Life

Choose one or more activities to bring the Bible to life.

Followers' Folly

Supplies: none

Zillies: hose

Create a soft ring using one of the **hose.** Slip your arm into the hose up to your elbow. Begin rolling the hose down toward your wrist. As you roll the hose, a ring will begin to form. Pull the ring up to your upper arm and continue. Do this until the hose forms a soft ring.

Select one student to be Jesus. Slip the soft ring on a hose. Tie the hose around Jesus' waist so that the ring is in the back. Make sure the hose is not too tight or too loose. It should neither cut off a boy or girl's circulation nor come off when tugged. Give each of the other students a hose.

Say: Let's play followers' folly. Jesus is going to try to tag you and ask you to become his (or her) follower. When Jesus tags you, he (or she) will say: "Follow me." Then you become a follower and slip your hose through the soft ring on Jesus' back. Then you must follow Jesus wherever he (or she) goes to tag others.

Give the students boundaries for the game. Continue playing until all of the students have been tagged and are following Jesus.

Say: Jesus knew that Levi was a dishonest tax collector. But Jesus knew that Levi could be a good person and could become a follower of Jesus. Jesus showed love to all people, even the sinners. Every person can be a follower of Jesus.

Levi's Lesson

Supplies: Reproducibles 9A and 9B

Zillies: none

Read or tell the story "Levi, The Tax Guy" **(Reproducibles 9A and 9B). Ask:** Why do you think things didn't feel quite right to Levi? What did Levi mean when he said he had been a Christian but not a follower? What happened that changed Levi's life? What kinds of experiences have you had that have helped you to be a follower of Jesus? If you were Levi, what would you do?

> **Every person can be a follower of Jesus.**

Life Zone

Choose one or more activities to bring the Bible to life.

Supplies:
Reproducible 9E, cassette player

Zillies:
Cassette

Sing

Give each student a copy of the words to the song "I Have Decided to Follow Jesus" **(Reproducible 9E).** Play the song on the **Cassette** and and ask the students to follow along. Play the song again and invite them to sing with you.

Say: Levi had been a tax collector. He was despised by everyone. Yet when Jesus saw him, Jesus asked Levi to follow him. Jesus loves all persons, regardless of who they are or what they have done. Levi gave up a job that made him a lot of money. He left everything and followed Jesus.

Supplies:
Reproducible 9D, pencils, caryons, tape, gold pencils or pens

Zillies:
gold coins

Money Rub

Give each student a copy of the coin art **(Reproducible 9D),** a **gold coin,** sharpened pencils, and crayons. Suggest they put a loop of tape on the table and press the gold coin onto the tape. Tell them to place the paper over the gold coin and rub the side of the pencil or crayon over the paper to make the impression of the coin. Encourage them to move the paper to do several coin rubbings around the coin. Have gold pencils, or pens available for them to add color to the large coin and the Bible verse.

Ask the students to say today's Bible verse: "Jesus said to him, 'Follow me.' And he got up, left everything, and followed him" (Luke 5:27b, 28, adapted). **Say: Money no longer meant anything to Levi. He gave up everything and followed Jesus.**

Supplies:
none

Zillies:
none

Sign 'n Pray

Teach the students how to sign the words "follow me." **Pray: Dear God, Jesus said,** (sign follow me). **We will follow. Amen.**

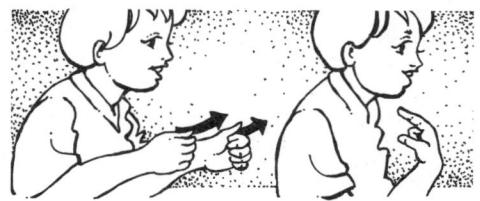

follow   me

Give each student a copy of HomeZone to enjoy this week.

Home Zone For Students

Money Wise

Jesus asked Levi to follow him. One way we can be followers of Jesus is to help others. Decide how much money you could save each week to give to a special cause. You can make a one-of-a-kind bank to save your money in.

Find a clean jar, bottle, or can that has a shape you like. Select bright colors of tissue paper. Twist, crumple, or braid the tissue paper or use flat strips. Pour glue into a bowl. Add just a little water to thin the glue.

Brush some glue on the jar. Lay a piece of tissue paper on the glue, then paint over the tissue paper with more glue. Continue painting glue on the jar, adding a piece of tissue paper, and painting the tissue paper with glue. You can overlap the pieces or add several layers. Cover the jar completely.

Let the jar dry thoroughly before you begin dropping your coins in it to save.

ThinkZone

Levi left everything to follow Jesus. Are there habits or attitudes you would have to change or "leave" to be a follower of Jesus?

Funny Face Followers

Make a fun dessert to serve your family. Select your favorite flavor of gelatin. Pour the gelatin into a bowl, add 1 cup boiling water, and stir with a rubber scraper until the gelatin is completely dissolved. Add 1 cup cold water. Stir until it is mixed well.

Use a large spoon to scoop the gelatin into four dessert dishes. Put the dishes in the refrigerator and let them chill until the gelatin is firm (about four hours).

Decorate the gelatin to create funny face followers. Use sprinkles or chocolate chips, or marshmallows for hair. Use coconut for beards, grapes for eyes, and pieces of licorice for eyelashes and mustaches. Use strawberry slices for noses and mouths and orange slices or mandarin oranges for ears.

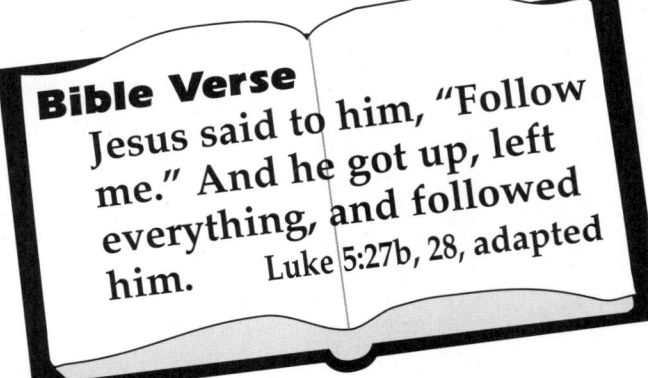

Bible Verse

Jesus said to him, "Follow me." And he got up, left everything, and followed him. Luke 5:27b, 28, adapted

Every person can be a follower of Jesus.

Older Elementary 3

Reproducible 9D

Permission granted to photocopy for local church use. © 1998 Abingdon Press.

Song Zone

I Have Decided to Follow Jesus

I have decided to follow Jesus;
I have decided to follow Jesus;
I have decided to follow Jesus;
No turning back, no turning back.

Tho 'none will join me, still I will follow;
Tho' none will join me, still I will follow;
Tho' none will join me, still I will follow;
No turning back, no turning back.

The world behind me, the cross before me;
The world behind me, the cross before me;
The world behind me, the cross before me;
No turning back, no turning back.

No turning back, no
No turning back, now, no turning back now.

I have decided to follow Jesus;
I have decided to follow Jesus;
I have decided to follow Jesus;
No turning back, no turning back.

I have decided to follow Jesus;
I have decided to follow Jesus;
I have decided to follow Jesus;
No turning back, no turning back.

Arr. © 1995 Bridge Building Music, Inc. (BMI), admin. by Brentwood-Benson Music Pubishing, Inc. All Rights Reserved. Used by permission.

Reproducible 9E
Permission granted to photocopy for local church use. © 1998 Abingdon Press.

10 Bible Zone

Jesus, Mary, and Martha

Enter the Zone

Bible Verse
Teach me your ways, O LORD; make them known to me.

Psalm 25:4, *Good News Bible*

Bible Story
Luke 10:38-42

The Scriptures tell us that Jesus had devout followers who were women. We do not know the names of all of them, but Mary, Martha, Mary Magdalene, Joanna, and Susanna are familiar names.

According to John 11:1–12:8 Mary and Martha were sisters who lived in Bethany, a village in Judea, near Jerusalem. Their brother was Lazarus, whom Jesus raised from the dead. Jesus' visit to the home of Mary and Martha suggests that he valued their friendship and accepted them in his ministry. His appreciation of them was a radical departure from the norm of society at that time. Women were considered to have little or no status and were often treated as outcasts. Instead, Jesus welcomed the women to listen to him and to learn from him, rather than relegating them to the role of serving men.

Luke 10:38-42 tells us that Jesus went to the house of Mary and Martha while traveling in southern Galilee. Martha apparently was the oldest and had responsibility for running the household. Martha busied herself with cooking and serving, while her sister Mary sat at Jesus' feet listening intently to him. When Martha complained to Jesus that Mary was not helping, he gently told her that she was too busy with less important, non-essential things.

Jesus' reply to Martha was not intended to say that he did not appreciate her hard work and sincere effort to prepare the meal and care for guests. Jesus wanted Martha to understand the difference between serving and ministering.

The two forms of hospitality in this story—serving and listening—have much to teach us about living a Christian life. Active Christianity and meditative Christianity are both important, and both have their own place. In this particular situation, Jesus told Martha that Mary had chosen the better form.

We can learn from Jesus.

Scope the Zone

ZONE	TIME	SUPPLIES	ZILLIES™
Zoom Into the Zone			
Get in the Zone	5 minutes	page 174, cassette player	Cassette
Listen 'n Twist	10 minutes	Reproducible 10C; red, blue, green, and yellow construction paper; scissors; markers; tape	slide flute
BibleZone™			
Zoom Into the Bible	10 minutes	Bible for each student	none
Get It From Both Sides	15 minutes	Reproducibles 10A and 10B	none
LifeZone			
Friendly Ties	15 minutes	Reproducible 10D, heavy tape OR thick cardboard and pushpins, six colors of yarn or embroidery thread	none
And the Leader Is?	10 minutes	none	none
Piggyback Fun	10 minutes	large piece of paper, small slips of paper, marker, basket, tape	none
Praise 'n Promise	10 minutes	Reproducible 10E, cassette player, large piece of paper, markers or crayons	Cassette

Zillies™ are found in the **BibleZone™ FUNspirational™ Kit.**

Zoom Into the Zone

Choose one or more activities to catch your children's interest.

Supplies:
page 174, cassette player

Zillies:
Cassette

Get in the Zone

Give each student a happy greeting. Have "The Bible Zone" playing on the **Cassette**. Invite the students to sing with you. Have copies of the words available **(page 174)** in case anyone needs them.

Supplies:
Reproducible 10C; red, blue, green, and yellow construction paper; scissors; markers; tape

Zillies:
slide flute

Listen 'n Twist

Have four sheets each of red, green, blue, and yellow construction paper. Draw a smiley face on each of the yellow and green sheets. Draw a heart on each of the red and blue sheets of paper.

Clear a large floor space. Arrange the sheets twelve inches apart in the following order to be used as a gameboard. Tape the sheets to the floor.

Line 1: red heart, yellow smiley face, blue heart, green smiley face
Line 2: yellow smiley face, blue heart, green smiley face, red heart
Line 3: blue heart, green smiley face, red heart, yellow smiley face
Line 4: green smiley face, red heart, yellow smiley face, blue heart

Cut out the strips that have the directions printed on them **(Reproducible 10C)**. Place the strips in a basket.

Ask everyone to take off his or her shoes and stand around the gameboard. **Say: This game is a little like Twister. I will draw a piece of paper from the basket and read the directions on the paper to you. Then I will use the slide flute. The paper will tell you the color, heart or smiley face, and right or left hand or foot. You must listen carefully so you can follow directions. The directions will tell you the color to touch, whether to touch the heart or the smiley face, and whether to use your foot or your hand to touch. There can be more than one person on the color.**

Draw the strips of directions and lead the students in the game for several minutes. Then ask them to sit down. **Ask: What did you have to do to play this game?** *(Listen carefully.)* **What happened sometimes?** *(People made mistakes because it was hard to listen.)*

Say: In today's Bible story we will find out why listening is so important.

Choose one or more activities to immerse your children in the Bible story.

Zoom Into the Bible

Be certain each student has a Bible. Ask everyone to read Luke 10:38-42.

Say: Jesus traveled through Galilee teaching, preaching, and healing. Some of the women supported Jesus' ministry by providing lodging and by feeding the disciples. The verses you have read tell us about Mary and Martha, who were friends of Jesus. Jesus had been traveling and stopped at their home.

Ask: What happened during the visit?

Supplies:
Bible for each student

Zillies:
none

Get It From Both Sides

Read or tell the story "A Tale of Two Sisters" **(Reproducibles 10A and 10B)**. (For tips about storytelling see the article on pages 171 and 172.)

Divide the class into two teams. Have the teams sit in chairs facing one another. Name one team "Mary's Team" and the other "Martha's Team." Ask the following questions and allow each team a time to answer. Encourage more than yes or no answers. **Ask:**

1. What kind of personality do you think Martha had?
2. Why do you think Martha was so worried about the appearance of the house and the food?
3. Do you think Martha was wrong to feel this way?
4. What did Jesus mean when he told Martha she was worrying about the wrong things?
5. Do you think Jesus appreciated how hard Martha had been working?
6. What else could Martha have done instead of complaining to Jesus? *(If she was upset, she could have talked to Mary privately.)*
7. What kind of personality do you think Mary had?
8. Why do you think only Mary cared about what Jesus was saying?
9. Do you think it was fair for Mary not to help Martha?
10. What did Jesus mean when he said Mary had chosen the right path?
11. Why did Jesus want Mary to listen to him?
12. What else could Mary have done that might have helped the situation? *(asked Martha to come and listen and offered to help her after Jesus had talked with them)*

Supplies:
Reproducibles 10A and 10B

Zillies:
none

Bible Zone Story

A Tale of Two Sisters
by Michael Williams

Mary speaks:

You can't understand if you don't have a sister like Martha. Now don't get me wrong. I love my sister, but she can be a real pain to live with sometimes. Even when we were little girls, she was cleaner and more organized than most grown-ups. She always had her homework done on time and her papers were done ahead of time. She kept her room so clean that you could eat off the floor. Except that she has always been so proper that she would never let you do something weird like that. For Martha cleanliness really is next to godliness, while for me cleanliness is next to impossible. We couldn't be more different if we were from different planets. I don't know how we wound up in the same family, unless that is God's way of making a joke, picking two people who are exactly the opposite to be sisters.

So I wasn't surprised when Martha spent the whole week cooking and cleaning up before our friend Jesus came. I thought the house was clean enough before she started, but she wanted it spotless. And the hard part was that she wanted me to want it to be as spotless as she did. I think some people just have different ideas about what clean is. I tried to help, I really did, but Martha could see dirt where I couldn't see anything.

Martha got irritated with me and accused me of daydreaming. But I wasn't daydreaming. I was remembering the stories Jesus had told us when he had visited before. I tried to remember every story, every detail of every story. All my sister could think about were the cobwebs in the corners and dust on the drapes. I kept telling her that this is Judea. We live in a house made of mud with a dirt floor. We're only going to get it so clean. Have you ever met anybody who thought she could make a dirt floor shine? Well, I have.

On the day we expected Jesus to arrive, I woke early and watched all morning. My sister kept saying, "A watched pot never boils," whatever that's supposed to mean. Then she kept sending me on errands. *Go get this. Run fetch that.* All I wanted to do was wait by the door and watch. Finally, after I had brought her everything that wasn't nailed down in the entire village of Bethany, Martha left me alone.

When Jesus finally came, I could hardly speak I was so excited, but at least I welcomed him in and saw that we extended the hospitality you are supposed to show a visiting rabbi. Martha was so busy in the kitchen that she hardly had a word to say to anyone, even Jesus. She was banging the pots and pans around so loudly that I had to sit close by his feet and listen very carefully to hear the stories Jesus was telling. She even tried to make Jesus tell me to get up and help her, but he wouldn't do it. He told her that I had chosen the better path and that she should not worry so much. He spoke to my sister in such a quiet, gentle voice that I could tell he was just concerned about her overdoing things and harming her health.

After she left the room, Jesus asked me if I knew how blessed I was to have a sister like Martha, and I said I did. The house does always look so nice when he comes and the meals are always so good. I know all that takes a lot of work and it is clear that Jesus enjoys everything that Martha does around here. Maybe that's why he loves her so much.

Martha speaks:

You wouldn't understand if you don't have a sister like Mary. Now don't get me wrong, I love my sister, but she can be a real pain to live with sometimes. Even when we were little girls, she was always dreaming up songs, stories, and ideas to impress our parents. They always thought she was so cute and so smart, even when her room looked like the Roman army had just camped there and left all their trash behind. No, Mary would walk around as if she was in some other world with a dreamy-eyed expression on her face. She acts like she thinks that she's some kind of poet or something. I have no earthly idea how two such different sisters came from the same two parents. Maybe God thinks we have something to learn from each other. If that is the case, it's the most exasperating lesson I have ever had.

So I wasn't surprised when Mary spent almost the whole week before Jesus arrived walking around in a daze. I would send her for water, then half an hour later find her leaning against the doorpost of our house staring off into space. When I would ask her about the water, she would say, "Oh, did you want me to get you some water?" I could hardly get my own work done (and believe me, there was plenty of work to be done) for having to look after her so that she did her little part. Mary can't even see piles of dirt when they are right there staring her in the face. I try to remind her gently that just because a floor is made of hard-packed earth doesn't mean it can't be clean. Well, as you might have guessed, I had to do all the cooking and cleaning and preparation for Jesus' visit. Believe me, if you want something done right in this house, you have to do it yourself.

On the morning Jesus was scheduled to arrive, Mary was even less help than usual. She just kept staring off in the direction from which Jesus would come. I tried to tell her that if she kept busy the time would pass faster and that he would be here before she knew it, but she didn't seem to hear a word I said. When Jesus finally did arrive, I was in the middle of the most difficult part of the meal and could have used some help. But did Mary even offer to help me? Did she even glance my way so I could give her a sign that I needed her? Not on your life. She just sat at Jesus' feet staring up into his eyes, hanging on his every word. Finally I had to go into the room and ask Jesus to tell her to come help me, and do you know what he said? He told me to settle down and not to worry so much. He said that Mary had chosen the better way to go, whatever that means. If somebody doesn't worry about these things, then he and Mary won't have anything to eat when they finally finish with their stories and are hungry.

Later Jesus asked me if I knew how blessed I was to have a sister like Mary. I know he enjoys having her hear and remember everything he says. She really is a good student and loves to learn everything Jesus has to teach. Maybe that's the reason he loves her so much.

Right foot, yellow smiley face. Right hand, blue heart.	Right hand, yellow smiley face. Right foot, blue heart.
Left foot, red heart. Left hand, yellow smiley face.	Left hand, red heart. Left foot, yellow smiley face.
Right foot, green smiley face. Left foot, red heart.	Right hand, green smiley face. Left foot, red heart.
Right hand, blue heart. Left foot, yellow smiley face.	Right hand, blue heart. Right foot, yellow smiley face.
Right foot, green smiley face. Right hand, blue heart.	Right foot, green smiley face. Left hand, blue heart.
Left foot, yellow smiley face. Left hand, green smiley face.	Right foot, yellow smiley face. Left hand, green smiley face.
Right foot, red heart. Left hand, blue heart.	Right hand, red heart. Left foot, blue heart.
Right hand, yellow smiley face. Left hand, red heart.	Right foot, yellow smiley face. Left hand, red heart.
Left foot, green smiley face. Left hand, red heart.	Left foot, green smiley face. Left hand, blue heart.

Reproducible 10C

Permission granted to photocopy for local church use. © 1998 Abingdon Press.

BibleZone™

Life

Choose one or more activities to bring the Bible to life.

Friendly Ties

Say: **Jesus taught Mary and Martha about God and God's love. He was their friend and showed them how he cared for them. We can show our friends how we care for them by making a gift for them. When you give your friend your gift, tell him or her about God and God's love.**

Give each student a copy of the instructions for making friendship bracelets **(Reproducible 10D)**. Have enough colors of yarn or embroidery thread available that each student will have six colors. Have either heavy tape or a piece of thick cardboard and a pushpin for each student.

Show the students how to put six strands of thread together and tie a knot in one end of the strands. Use a pushpin to pin the knot to a piece of cardboard so that the thread can be laid out on the cardboard. Or use heavy tape and tape the knot to the top of the table. Guide the students step by step in making the bracelets.

Supplies:
Reproducible 10D, heavy tape OR thick cardboard and pushpins, six colors of yarn or embroidery thread

Zillies:
none

And the Leader Is?

Ask the students to sit in a circle. Select one student to leave the room. Say: **In this game one person will go outside the room. Everyone inside the room will select a secret leader. The leader will create a pattern of clapping hands, snapping fingers, and stomping feet for the group to follow. The person who is outside the room must come back in and watch the group and try to guess who the leader is. If the leader is discovered, he or she goes outside the room, and a new secret leader is chosen.**

Play the game until all the students have been secret leaders. Say: **We learn all the time. Because we are constantly learning, sometimes it is hard for us to realize who is teaching us. The most important thing we can remember is that we can learn from Jesus how we should live.**

Supplies:
none

Zillies:
none

 **We can learn from Jesus.**

Older Elementary 3

Life Zone

Choose one or more activities to bring the Bible to life.

Supplies:
large piece of paper, small slips of paper, marker, basket, tape

Zillies:
none

Piggyback Fun

Write today's Bible verse on a large piece of paper and put it where everyone can see it. Write the following song titles on slips of paper, fold the slips, and put them in a basket: "The Farmer in the Dell," "Mary Had a Little Lamb," and "She'll Be Coming Around the Mountain." Prepare enough slips so that there is one for each student. Make sure you use the same song at least twice.

Pass the basket around and ask each student to take one slip. **Say: After you read the name of the song on your slip of paper, do not say anything. Start humming the song that is written on the slip. While you are humming, walk around the room and find others who are humming the same song. Divide into groups according to the song you are humming.**

Ask the groups to work together to create a song using the words of the Bible verse to the tune of the song they were humming. Then ask each group to teach its song to the class and have everyone sing together.

Supplies:
Reproducible 10E, cassette player, large piece of paper, markers or crayons

Zillies:
Cassette

Praise 'n Promise

Give each student a copy of the words to the song "Is There Anything I Can Do for You?" **(Reproducible 10E)**. Play the song on the **Cassette** and ask the students to follow along as they listen to the song. Play the song again and invite them to sing with you.

Write "WCWDFJ?" on a large piece of paper. Put the paper on the wall. Give each student a marker or crayon. **Say: We can learn from Jesus. Jesus teaches us how to love our friends. Jesus teaches us how much God loves us. Jesus teaches us how we should live. The question is: What can we do for Jesus? What can we do with the things Jesus teaches us?** Ask the students to write their answers on the paper.

Pray: Thank you, God, for Jesus. Thank you for the things Jesus teaches us. Help us to listen carefully so we can learn. Help us to understand so we can use what we learn to help others know and love you. Amen.

We can learn from Jesus.

Give each student a copy of HomeZone to enjoy this week.

Home Zone For Students

A Great Glass Band

Listening is something we can learn to do better and better. Make your own glass band to practice listening.

You will need three glasses (the ones with thin glass make the best sound, but ask your parents first!). Fill one glass ¼ full, one glass ½ full, and one glass ¾ full of water.

Use a metal spoon and gently tap the sides of the glass to make a sound.

You actually can play a song on the glasses! Think of the glass with the most water as number 3 and the glass with the least water as number 1. Number the other glass 2. Tap the glasses in the following order to play "Mary Had a Little Lamb":

```
3 2 1 2 3 3 3
  2 2 2 3 3 3
3 2 1 2 3 3 3
  3 2 2 3 2 1
```

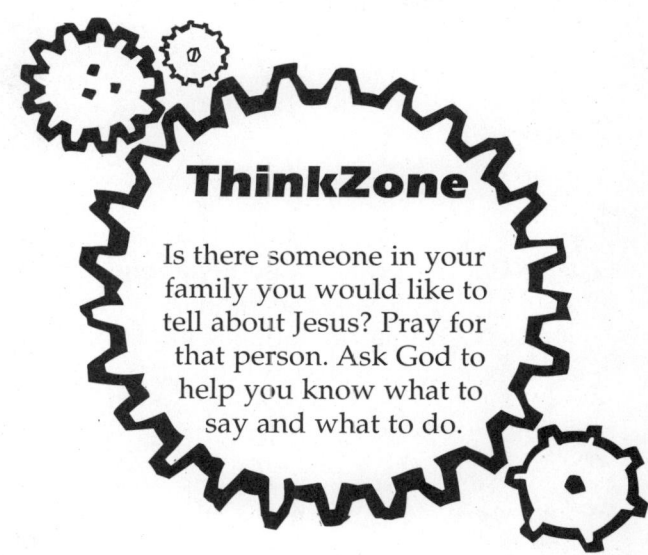

ThinkZone

Is there someone in your family you would like to tell about Jesus? Pray for that person. Ask God to help you know what to say and what to do.

People Chow

Make a fun snack to share with your friends. You will need:

12 ounces semi-sweet chocolate chips
1 stick margarine
½ cup peanut butter
12 ounces Rice Chex cereal
2 cups powdered sugar

Melt the margarine in a saucepan. Add the peanut butter and chocolate chips and stir them together until everything is melted and mixed together. Remove the pan from the stove.

Add the Rice Chex cereal and mix thoroughly. Put the powdered sugar in a plastic sealable bag. Scoop the mixture into the bag and toss it all together. Store the people chow in an airtight container.

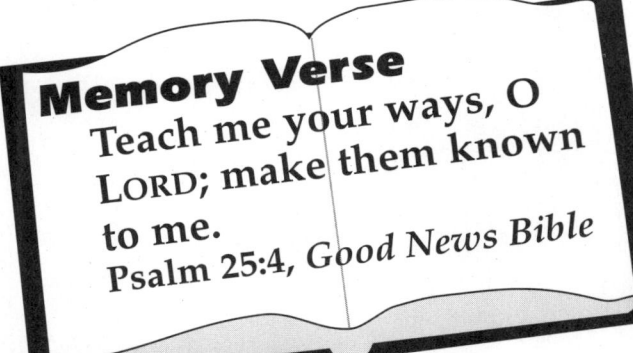

Memory Verse

Teach me your ways, O LORD; make them known to me.
Psalm 25:4, *Good News Bible*

We can learn from Jesus.

Permission granted to photocopy for local church use. © 1998 Abingdon Press.

OLDER ELEMENTARY 3

Friendship Bracelets

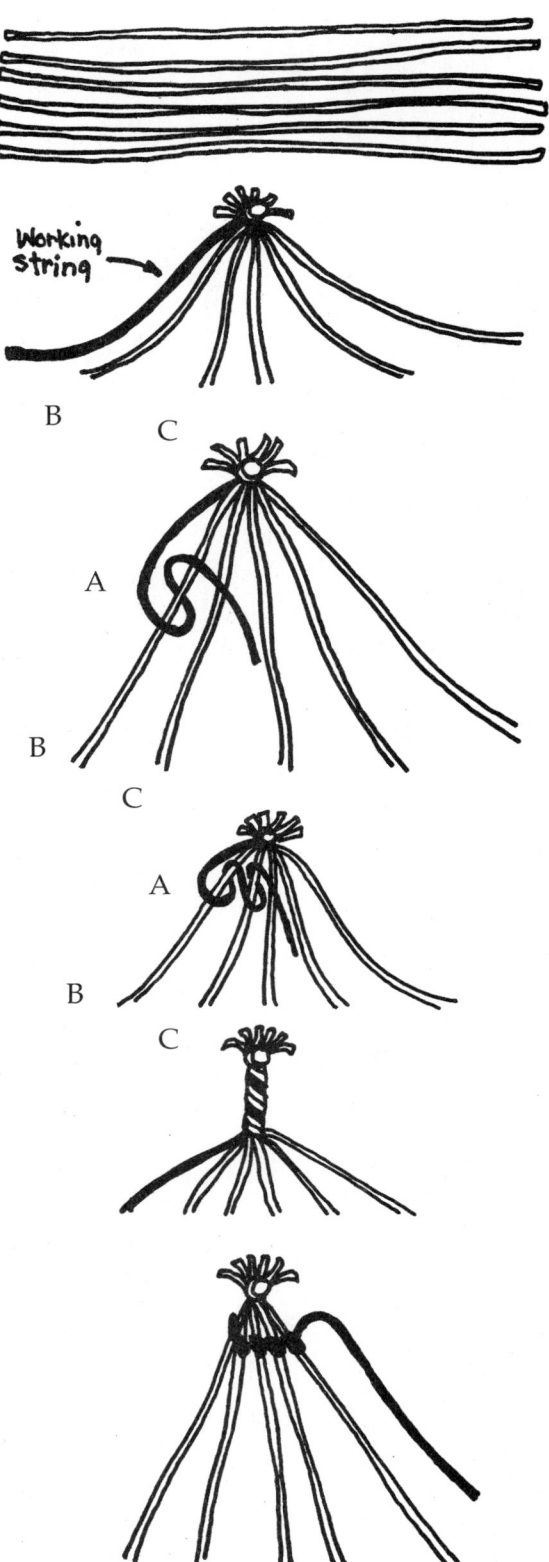

1. Cut six strands of different colors of yarn or embroidery thread four times the length you want your bracelet to be.

2. Knot the strands together at one end. Push a pushpin through the knot and into a piece of thick cardboard. Or you can tape the knot to the top of a table to hold it in place.

3. Use the first strand on the left as the "working strand." The working strand is A in the picture. Hold the working strand (A) in one hand. Hold strand B in the other hand stretched enough to keep it tight. Make a knot shaped like a 4 by going across strand B and then back under it, and back across where you first crossed it. Pull the working strand (A) up to the top to make a knot. Repeat these instructions to make a second knot.

4. Repeat the instructions, but this time make strand C the one you use with the working string. Repeat again to make a second knot.

5. Repeat across all the colors using the same working strand. Be sure to make two knots with each color. Continue until you have a diagonal stripe of the working strand.

6. Begin a second row. Strand B is now the first strand and has become the working strand. Repeat the directions for steps 3-6. Then begin the third row with Strand C as the working strand. Continue until all the strands have been used.

Reproducible 10D

Permission granted to photocopy for local church use. © 1998 Abingdon Press.

BibleZone™

Song Zone

Is There Anything I Can Do For You?

Is there anything I can do for you?
Is there anything I can do?
For all the things you've done for me,
Is there anything I can do?
I'm willing to be used, dear Lord,
What e'er the price may be.
So if there's anything I can do for you,
just make it known to me.

Is there anywhere I can go for you?
Is there anywhere I can go?
For the places you have been for me,
Is there anywhere I can go?
I'm willing to be used, dear Lord,
Whate'er the price may be.
So if there's anywhere I can go for you,
just make it known to me.
Just make it known to me.

© 1977 by John T. Benson Publishing (ASCAP)/Bridge Building Music, Inc. (BMI), admin. by Brentwood-Benson Music Publishing, Inc. All rights reserved. Used by permission.

11 Bible

Jesus and Zacchaeus

Enter the

Bible Verse
For the Son of Man came to seek out and to save the lost.

Luke 19:10

Bible Story
Luke 19:1-10

Under the rule of the Romans in the time of Jesus, the people of Judea were required to pay numerous taxes—a tax on the soil, a poll tax, and a tax on personal property, as well as import and export duties. The privilege of collecting the taxes was auctioned to the highest bidder, generally a wealthy Roman, who in turned hired tax collectors to do the actual work of collecting the revenues. It was understood that these tax collectors could charge an amount over the actual tax in order to pay for their labors and the risk involved in their job. The tax collectors often abused the privilege by collecting amounts of money that greatly exceeded the amount owed. As a result, tax collectors were hated and considered no better than robbers and murderers. Tax collectors were not permitted to worship in the synagogue.

The Scriptures hint that Zacchaeus was not a tall person. Being a despised tax collector, Zacchaeus may well have climbed the tree to overcome the obstacles of his height and to avoid the unsympathetic crowd. Obviously Zacchaeus truly felt the need to see Jesus. When Jesus called him out of the sycamore tree, the people watching must have been shocked. Jesus treated Zacchaeus with honor by staying in his home and eating with him. Jesus challenged the people to a new kind of love when he openly accepted the fellowship of people who were considered sinners.

Jesus' loving actions had a life-changing effect on Zacchaeus. Zacchaeus responded by showing compassion to the people he had wronged. He repaid them four times what he had taken from them. Not only did Zacchaeus find a way to see Jesus, he found a way to be what Jesus called him to be—a loving and caring person. The story of Zacchaeus illustrates God's love for all people, in all walks of life, and how God wants us to love one another.

Jesus loves and accepts everyone.

Scope the

ZONE	TIME	SUPPLIES	ZILLIES™
Zoom Into the Zone			
Get in the Zone	5 minutes	page 174, cassette player	Cassette
Z-Find	15 minutes	Bibles, Reproducible 11D, crayons, markers	none
Cheater's Challenge	10 minutes	none	sponge balls
BibleZone™			
Zoom Into the Zone	15 minutes	Bible for each student, Reproducible 11C, two bags, paper and marker	none
Dig Into the Story	15 minutes	Reproducibles 11A and 11B	none
LifeZone			
Poor Lefty!	10 minutes	dish of M&M candies	slide flute
B-I-B-L-E Ball	20 minutes	Reproducible 11C, scissors, tape, two chairs	sponge balls, net square
Lost & Found	20 minutes	Reproducible 11E, cassette player, leisure and news magazines, glue or glue-sticks, large piece of paper	Cassette

⊙ Zillies™ are found in the **BibleZone™ FUNspirational™ Kit.**

OLDER ELEMENTARY 3

Zoom Into the Zone

Choose one or more activities to catch your children's interest.

Supplies:
page 174, cassette player

Zillies:
Cassette

Get in the Zone

Greet the students with genuine enthusiasm. Have the song "The Bible Zone" playing on the **Cassette.** Invite the students to sing with you. Have copies of the words to the song **(page 174)** available in case anyone needs them.

Supplies:
Bibles, Reproducible 11D, crayons, markers

Zillies:
none

Z-Find

Ask the students to name everything they can think of that starts with the letter Z. If they name Zacchaeus, **ask: Who was he? What did he do?**

If the students do not name Zacchaeus, **say: The Bible tells us about a man named Zacchaeus who wanted to see Jesus so badly that he did something very unusual.**

Give each student a copy of the biblical art **(Reproducible 11D)**. Ask everyone to find Zacchaeus and Jesus in the picture. Tell the students they may read Luke 19:4 if they cannot find Jesus and Zacchaeus. Invite the students to color the picture if they are waiting for other classmates to arrive.

Supplies:
none

Zillies:
sponge balls

Cheater's Challenge

Have all the students stand in a circle. **Say: I will throw a sponge ball in the air. Let's see who can catch it.**

Toss the ball into the air. Ask the student who catches the ball to stand in the middle of the circle. **Say: You will be Zacchaeus. Zacchaeus was a man who lived in Bible times. People thought Zacchaeus was a disgusting tax collector who cheated everyone.**

Toss two **sponge balls** into the circle. **Say: The object of this game is for you to kick the ball and hit Zacchaeus with it. All hits must be below the waist. Zacchaeus is going to try to dodge the balls. The person who hits Zacchaeus with the ball becomes Zacchaeus and stands in the middle of the circle.**

BIBLEZONE™

Bible

Choose one or more activities to immerse your children in the Bible story.

Zoom Into the Zone

Be certain each student has a Bible. Divide the students into two teams. Ask Team One to read Luke 19:1-6. Ask Team Two to read Luke 19:7-10.

Photocopy and cut out the cards marked Team One and Team Two **(upper half, Reproducible 11C)** and put them in separate bags. Give each team its bag.

Say: Each bag contains eight words. Use those eight words to tell the part of the Bible story you read. Use each word as often as you can. I will keep score to see which team uses their words the most.

Supplies:
Bible for each student, Reproducible 11C, two bags, paper and marker

Zillies:
none

Dig Into the Story

Read or tell the story "An Uncommon Thief" **(Reproducibles 11A and 11B).** (For great storytelling tips read the article on pages 171–172.) Ask the following questions. Encourage conversation rather than yes or no answers.

1. What kind of a person was Zacchaeus?
2. Why do you suppose Zacchaeus wanted to see Jesus?
3. How do you think Zacchaeus felt about being in that crowd of people?
4. What would you think if you saw a man like Zacchaeus crawl up a tree?
5. Why do you think the people were excited about seeing Jesus?
6. What do you suppose they were thinking when Jesus stopped to speak to Zacchaeus?
7. Why do you think Jesus invited himself to Zacchaeus's house?
8. What did Zacchaeus decide to do after Jesus spoke to him?
9. Why do you think Zacchaeus decided that?
10. Have you ever known anyone like Zacchaeus?
11. How would Jesus treat that person?
12. How would Jesus want you to treat that person?

Supplies:
Reproducibles 11A and 11B

Zillies:
none

 **Jesus loves and accepts everyone.**

OLDER ELEMENTARY 3

Bible Zone Story

An Uncommon Thief
by Michael Williams

Zacchaeus was not your ordinary, run-of-the-mill thief. He was a tax collector. In the time of Jesus, being a tax collector practically gave a person a license to steal. This is how it worked. The Roman government told each tax collector to collect a certain amount of money from his people. Anything more that the tax collector dared to collect went to him and became his salary. A tax collector could make as much money as he wanted, as long as he didn't mind stealing it from his people.

Zacchaeus didn't seem to mind stealing from his own people. You see, Zacchaeus became very rich by not minding stealing from his neighbors. In the process his neighbors in Jericho learned to hate Zacchaeus. He was like the playground bully. You know as well as I do that nobody likes the playground bully, nobody. Zacchaeus was an uncommon bully, though.

This is why Jesus' behavior was so strange that day he came to Jericho. Everybody and his dog turned out that day. No, I really mean it. There were about as many dogs as people. The crowd was so thick around Jesus that there was no way for children and short adults even to get a glimpse of the visiting rabbi. Zacchaeus wanted to see Jesus too. While the tax collector might be able to bully people into giving up their money, he couldn't bully his way in front of a single soul that day. No one was going to give up a choice spot to see Jesus, even if Zacchaeus promised that they wouldn't have to pay as much in taxes next year. Which he didn't even offer, by the way.

No, the Jericho bully had something up his sleeve. He found a nearby tree with limbs close enough to the ground that he could reach them and strong enough to hold his weight, and he climbed it. Now Zacchaeus was no youngster. To tell the truth, which Zacchaeus didn't do very often, he hadn't tried to climb a tree in years. In fact, the bully looked pretty silly holding up the skirts of his cloak, lifting skinny legs that were white as chalk, and carefully reaching from limb to limb. Before long he was perched in the middle of one of the stronger limbs. He looked like a hunting bird ready to swoop down and capture some unsuspecting mouse. His neighbors, who knew him better than they wanted to, knew he was capable of doing more harm than a bird on the attack.

It wasn't long before Jesus came along surrounded by his friends and followers. The crowd was so loud that no one except those closest to him could hear. Then Jesus stopped and looked around as if he was looking for someone in particular. Then the teacher lifted his arm and pointed toward the tree in which Zacchaeus sat. Was the visiting rabbi going to let the village bully have a piece of his mind? Was he going to shame the tax collector right in front of the people he had cheated? *This was going to be great*, they thought. "It's about time somebody told him off," they whispered to each other. The crowd was even more excited than when Jesus had arrived.

Then Jesus stopped under the tree where Zacchaeus sat. The teacher held up his hands for everyone to be quiet. He looked directly at the tax collector and told him to come down. Then the next thing the teacher said shocked us all. He told Zacchaeus that he was coming to his house to eat with him that very day.

Now to eat with someone is to forgive that person. We weren't sure that anyone, even Jesus, had the right to do anything to make that scoundrel think that what he had done was okay. Why would a rabbi, a respected teacher, pick out the worst person in Jericho and invite himself to dinner? Nobody could figure it out, and nobody liked it either. You would think that a good and wise teacher would pick someone good and wise to eat with.

Well, the strangest thing happened. As we all stood around grinding our teeth with anger, Zacchaeus slowly and carefully climbed down from the tree. When he was standing on the earth at last, he looked directly at Jesus and said something that was even more amazing. "Half of everything I own I will give to the poor," he began. I'm sure we all had our mouths hanging open in surprise hearing that. I happened to be looking at Jesus, and even he looked surprised. *Half of his fortune*, I was thinking. *That's fine for the poor, but what about all the hard-working middle-class citizens who had been cheated year after year? What about us*, I thought? *What do we get?*

No sooner had those questions entered my mind than Zacchaeus started to speak again. "If I have cheated anyone or taken anything that I did not deserve," he began. *If?* I thought. *If you have taken anything unfairly?* Every person standing in that crowd had been cheated in one way or another by this bully. I couldn't believe that he would have the nerve to say, "If I have cheated anyone."

The next words that came out of the tax collector's mouth struck me like someone had hit me in the stomach. "I will repay those persons four times what I took from them."

As soon as we could get over the shock of what we had heard, we all began to add up the tax we had been charged over the years and multiply by four. The totals we came up with were staggering. Could this scoundrel be telling the truth? Could Jesus' words, inviting himself to dinner, have caused such a big change so quickly?

Then the rabbi looked at the crowd and said, "Why were you so surprised that I invited myself to eat with Zacchaeus? He is as much a child of our ancestor Abraham as you are. Don't you see? I didn't come to save those who are saved already. I came to save the lost."

By the time I had taken in this sudden change of heart, I looked up and saw Jesus and Zacchaeus walking away toward the tax collector's house arm in arm. That is why I say that Zacchaeus was no ordinary tax collector. And Jesus, who offered that old bully forgiveness by inviting himself to dinner, what do I say about him? Well, that Jesus is no ordinary teacher.

Reproducible 11B

Permission granted to photocopy for local church use. © 1998 Abingdon Press.

Team One **Zacchaeus**	Team Two **Zacchaeus**
Team One **Jesus**	Team Two **Jesus**
Team One **short**	Team Two **sinner**
Team One **crowd**	Team Two **half**
Team One **tax collector**	Team Two **poor**
Team One **tree**	Team Two **four**
Team One **rich**	Team Two **save**
Team One **climb**	Team Two **lost**

- For the
- Son of
- Man came
- to seek
- out and
- to save
- the lost
- Luke 19:10

Reproducible 11C

Choose one or more activities to bring the Bible to life.

Poor Lefty!

Put a chair in the middle of the room. Ask everyone to stand around the chair in a circle. Ask a question that points out a unique feature of one student; for example, "Who has green eyes?" or "Who is wearing boots?" or "Who is wearing a white shirt?"

Go to whichever student responds, put your hands on his or her shoulder, and **say: Hello, Lefty.** Take that student out of the circle.

Have a small dish of M&M candies. Pass the dish around and **say: You may each have two pieces. But Lefty doesn't get any. Lefty is left out. Lefty is excluded.** After everyone has had the candy, place the bowl on the chair in the center of the circle.

Ask everyone standing in the circle to lock arms. **Say: Lefty is going to run around the circle and try to get under or through your arms so that (he or she) can have some candy too. I will use the slide flute to signal when to start and when to stop.**

Let Lefty try for a minute or two to get into the circle. Then use the **slide flute** to signal the students to stop. Ask another question to find a new Lefty. Pass the M&M candies around and begin the game again. Play until everyone has been Lefty. Pass the remaining candies around for everyone to enjoy.

Ask: How did it feel to be Lefty? What is so bad about being left out?

Say: Today we learned that Jesus loved and accepted Zacchaeus, even though Zacchaeus had been despised by everyone.

Ask: What is unfair about excluding people? Who should be left out? Who should be included? Why did Jesus include Zacchaeus?

 **Jesus loves and accepts everyone.**

Supplies:
dish of M&M candies

Zillies:
slide flute

Life

Choose one or more activities to bring the Bible to life.

Supplies:
Reproducible 11C, scissors, tape, two chairs

Zillies:
net square, sponge balls

B-I-B-L-E Ball

Cut out the Bible verse circles (**bottom half, Reproducible 11C**) and tape each one to a **sponge ball**. Read the words on the balls to the students so they may hear today's Bible verse in the correct order. Create a "basket" similar to one used on a basketball goal by attaching the **net square** to two chairs and positioning the chairs with some space between them.

Have eight students pick a number between one and eight without anyone selecting the same number. Ask them to line up in order according to the number they chose. Give each student a sponge ball. **Say: We are going to play B-I-B-L-E ball. Player #1 goes first and may toss the ball from anywhere in the room. If Player #1 makes the basket, then everyone else must toss the ball in numerical order from the same spot in the room. The first player who misses the basket gets the letter B. If Player #1 misses the basket, he or she gets the letter B, and Player #2 may take a shot from anywhere in the room. If all eight players make the basket, Player #1 may move to a new position in the room and shoot the ball. The game continues in this way, and each time you miss the basket, you get another letter from B-I-B-L-E. When you have gotten all the letters, you must borrow all the sponge balls and put them in order to read today's Bible verse.**

Continue the game until several students have said the Bible verse.

Supplies:
Reproducible 11E, cassette player, leisure and news magazines, glue or glue sticks, large piece of paper

Zillies:
Cassette

Lost & Found

Have pages showing pictures of people cut from several magazines. Include pictures from leisure and news magazines. Put a large piece of paper where everyone can reach it. Also have bottles of glue or glue sticks available for everyone to share. **Say: Jesus loves and accepts everyone. Jesus came to seek out and save the lost. Let's make a montage of people Jesus loves. Tear pictures from the magazine pages and glue them on the paper. The pictures may overlap.**

Play "I've Been Redeemed" on the **Cassette** while the students work. Have copies of the words (**Reproducible 11E**) available for anyone who wants to sing along. Pray, thanking God for Jesus in our lives.

Give each student a copy of HomeZone to enjoy this week.

BibleZone™

Home Zone For Students

Lost & Found

Begin a lost and found collection at home. Look in the newspaper and magazines for articles and pictures of people who are struggling and need either Jesus' healing or forgiveness. Make a lost and found poster using those pictures.

Take time each day to look at your poster and read about the people you chose. Pray for those people. Ask God's forgiveness for their sins. Ask God's healing for their problems or situations.

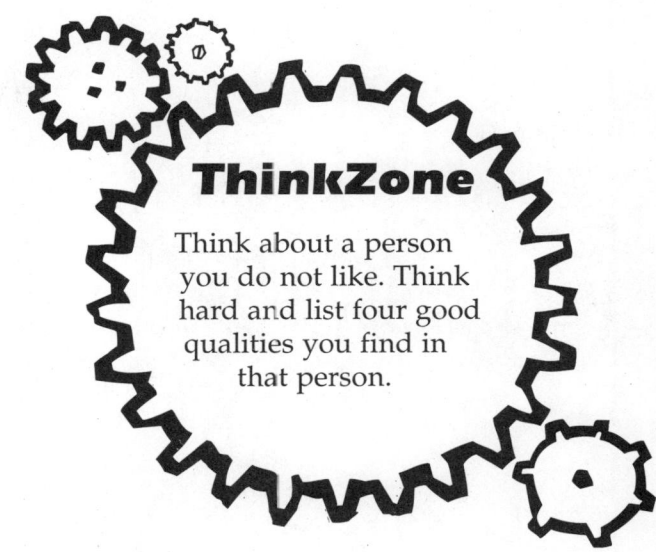

ThinkZone

Think about a person you do not like. Think hard and list four good qualities you find in that person.

Memory Verse

For the Son of Man came to seek out and to save the lost. Luke 19:10

Church Windows

You will need:
½ cup margarine (1 stick)
2 cups semisweet chocolate chips
1 cup chopped nuts
1 (10-ounce) package of colored miniature marshmallows
1 cup grated coconut

Combine the margarine and chocolate chips in a saucepan. Cook over low heat until they are melted. Cool slightly. Stir in the nuts and marshmallows. Shape into a log on waxed paper sprinkled with coconut. Be sure to get coconut all over the log.

Wrap the log in the waxed paper or cellophane paper. Put it in the freezer until it feels firm.

Slice the log into pieces and serve it to your family or friends.

 **Jesus loves and accepts everyone.**

Permission granted to photocopy for local church use. © 1998 Abingdon Press.

Song Zone

I've Been Redeemed

I've been redeemed by the blood of the Lamb.
I've been redeemed by the blood of the Lamb.
I've been redeemed by the blood of the Lamb,
I'm going to the promised land.
All my sins are washed away,
I've been redeemed.

God sent his son to die for me.
God sent his son to die for me.
God sent his son to die for me,
So I could live eternally.
All my sins are washed away,
I've been redeemed.

You can talk about me just all you please.
You can talk about me just all you please.
You can talk about me just all you please.
I'll talk about you when I'm on my knees.
All my sins are washed away cause
I've been redeemed

I'm on my way to Heaven above.
Gee I'm on my way to Heaven above.
I'm on my way to Heaven above.
I'm filled with God's fantastic love.
All my sins are washed away cause
 I've been redeemed

Arr. © 1996 New Spring Publishing, Inc. (ASCAP), admin. by Brentwood-Benson Music Publishing, Inc. All rights reserved. Used by permission.

Reproducible 11E

Permission granted to photocopy for local church use. © 1998 Abingdon Press.

12 Bible

The Woman at the Well

Enter the

Bible Verse
"Those who drink of the water that I will give them will never be thirsty."
John 4:14a

Bible Story
John 4:1-34, 39-42

When Jesus spoke to the Samaritan woman at the well, he was going against customary social practices for that time. Although they shared a common heritage, Samaritans and Jews differed greatly on several religious traditions and did not associate with each other. It was also customary for a rabbi to avoid speaking to a woman in public. As a Jew who often was called "rabbi" by his followers, Jesus should not have spoken to the woman at the well; the woman herself was surprised that he did.

Jesus spoke to the woman about living water, the kind that comes through him and quenches spiritual thirst. The woman did not fully understand him because she could not get past the physical need for water. It was only when Jesus told her what he knew of her background that she began to realize that something was different about Jesus. Even then, she thought he was a prophet. Finally she hesitantly referred to the Messiah, and Jesus confirmed that he was the Chosen One.

It is not surprising that the Samaritan woman did not realize at first with whom she was speaking. Even Jesus' disciples did not always understand what Jesus was trying to tell them.

Jesus brought a radical change to the religious practices of the day. Even though Jesus was the fulfillment of the Old Testament prophecy of the Messiah, God did not send Jesus exclusively for the Jews. Jesus came as Savior for all persons, bringing God's message of salvation to the whole world. The story of Jesus and the woman at the well is only one of several accounts of Jesus' disregard for established customs in favor of spreading his message to all people.

Jesus teaches us how to live in the presence of God.

Scope the Zone

ZONE	TIME	SUPPLIES	ZILLIES™
Zoom Into the Zone			
Get in the Zone	5 minutes	page 174, cassette player	Cassette
Wacky Walk	10 minutes	Reproducible 12D two small hand mirrors, bucket	slide flute
BibleZone™			
Zoom Into the Bible	10 minutes	Bible for each student	none
Dig Into the Story	20 minutes	Reproducibles 12A, 12B, and 12C	none
LifeZone			
Thirst Quenchers	5 minutes	salty crackers, water, cups	slide flute
Thirst Stoppers	15 minutes	two one-gallon jars of water, straws	slide flute
Bible Verse Smuggle	10 minutes	Reproducible 12C, scissors	slide flute
Sing	5 minutes	Reproducible 12E, cassette player	Cassette
Pray	5 minutes	small clean bucket, small cups, water	none

Zillies™ are found in the **BibleZone™ FUNspirational™ Kit.**

OLDER ELEMENTARY 3

Zoom Into the Zone

Choose one or more activities to catch your children's interest.

Supplies:
page 174, cassette player

Zillies:
Cassette

Get in the Zone

Have the song "The Bible Zone" **(Cassette)** playing as the students enter the room. Greet each student enthusiastically. Invite the students to sing with you. Have copies of the words **(page 174)** available for anyone who needs them.

Supplies:
Reproducible 12D, two small hand mirrors, bucket

Zillies:
slide flute

Wacky Walk

Plan to have this game in the largest space available. Have copies of the cards cut apart **(Reproducible 12D),** being sure that you have one card per student. Place the cards in a pile face down on a chair or small table. Also place two small hand mirrors on the table or chair. Make a sign that says "Well" and put it on the other side of the room. Place a bucket under the sign.

Divide the class into two teams. Have the teams line up with the chair or table in the middle. **Explain: I will give you a signal with the slide flute to begin. The first player from each team draws a card. That player must walk to the well. You have to walk the same way as the picture on the card you draw. When you get to the well, put your card in the bucket and stand beside the bucket. As soon as your card drops into the bucket, the next player on your team draws a card and begins his or her walk. As each of you drop your card in the bucket, join your teammate in line beside the bucket. The first team to line up beside the bucket wins. Remember! This is a walk, not a run!**

When the game is over, ask everyone to sit on the floor near the bucket. **Say:** Jesus walked through Palestine, meeting people and teaching them. He had been in Judea in southern Palestine and was going north to Galilee. On his way he went through Samaria and stopped in a town called Sychar. Jesus was tired from the walk, and he sat by the well. Often the well was a social place where people met and visited during their daily chores. While he was there, Jesus did something that was very unusual. Our Bible story today will tell us what happened.

Jesus teaches us how to live in the presence of God.

Bible

Choose one or more activities to immerse your children in the Bible story.

Zoom Into the Bible

Supplies: Bible for each student

Zillies: none

Be certain each student has a Bible. Ask the students to open their Bibles to John 4. **Say: This chapter of John tells us about Jesus and the woman at the well.**

Ask your students who enjoy reading aloud to take turns reading John 4:1-34, 39-42. Divide the number of verses for each student to read as equally as possible.

Dig Into the Story

Supplies: Reproducibles 12A, 12B, and 12C

Zillies: none

Tell or read the story "Echoes From the Well" **(Reproducibles 12A, 12B, and 12C).** (For great storytelling hints read the article on pages 171 and 172.).

Ask the following questions:
1. Why was the well such an important place in Bible times?
2. What important things happened at the well?
3. Why did the Jews and the Samaritans hate each other?
4. Why did people talk about the Samaritan woman?
5. How do you suppose the Samaritan woman felt when Jesus asked her to give him a drink of water?
6. How so you suppose the Samaritan woman felt when she discovered that Jesus knew everything about her?
7. What did Jesus mean when he said "those who drink of the water that I give them will never be thirsty?"
8. What do you think the woman had heard about the Messiah, who she said was coming?
9. Should the disciples have been upset with Jesus for speaking to the woman? Why or why not?
10. What was the food Jesus told his disciples about?

Say: Jesus used the words *living water* as a metaphor. A metaphor is a word that means one thing and is used to mean something else. Jesus knew the woman would understand the meaning of living water. The woman lived near Judea where there was desert. Knowing where water was could mean the difference between life and death. The living water Jesus spoke of was "water" that moves us toward God so we can live in the presence of God.

OLDER ELEMENTARY 3

Bible Zone Story

Echoes From the Well

by Michael Williams

Many people come to me day by day to draw water. Without that daily supply of water they could not live. The women of the village come early in the morning or late in the evening to get water for themselves and their families. One can live for some time without food, but not without water. I am a source of life for this village.

I am a source of history too. I am the well of our ancestor Jacob. I am the well who has been catching the words of the people who have come here from Jacob's time until now. I have heard the words of gossip by those who come here speaking about those who are not here. A well is one place people come to tell tales on their neighbors.

A well is also a place where love stories begin. Remember, both the bride of Jacob and the bride of his father Isaac were first met at wells. Many love stories start here. The story I have to tell you today is not a romance, but it is a love story. I will explain more about that later.

I sit at the foot of Mount Gerizim, the holy mountain of the Samaritans, not far from the ancient city of Shechem. Since the Jews worship God at Jerusalem and the Samaritans worship God on this mountain, Jews and Samaritans rarely talk to each other. In fact you could say that Jews and Samaritans hate each other. They worship the same God on two different mountains, yet they wind up hating each other. Go figure. I am deep but not deep enough to understand that.

That is why I want to tell you about what happened here today. It is so unusual. First, there is a woman who comes here during the middle of the day. Believe me, no one comes here in the heat of the day if they can help it. It is very hot and very uncomfortable. Still she comes every day at that time. If you ask me, I think she is hoping to avoid the other women. They do talk about her sometimes, but she is not here to hear their gossip about her. I guess she just doesn't want them to say anything mean to her face. You see, she has never had any children, and the people here think that is a shameful thing. They blame her for it. She has been divorced by one husband after another, I suppose because she couldn't give them children. Now she has been taken into the household of one who refuses to marry her. What would be the use, if she can't have children? Anyway, she comes to me in the heat of the day so she will not be reminded of her shame.

Today there was a man at the well when she arrived. He asked her for a drink of water. Now, it is unusual for a man to speak to a woman who is not his wife or daughter. Come to find out he is Jewish, and it is even more rare for a Jewish man to have anything to do with a Samaritan woman. It just doesn't happen. But it did, right here, this very day. She remarked that Jews and Samaritans won't even drink from the same cups. Then the man said the strangest thing. He told her that if she knew who she was talking to, she would ask him for water. She chuckled and pointed out that he didn't have a bucket and that I was deep.

Reproducible 12A

Permission granted to photocopy for local church use. © 1998 Abingdon Press.

Then the Jewish man, who was clearly a teacher, started talking about water he could give her, living water. Now, I don't know where he would find running water, what he calls living water, around here. I am the nearest watering place and my water just sits there. It's what you call still water.

He told her that if she drank of the water he could give her, she would never be thirsty again. The water he would give her would be like an ever-flowing fountain for a never ending life. Well, she said she would jump at the chance, but I wasn't so sure. If people could get a drink of water and never get thirsty again, I would be a very lonely well.

Then the visitor asked her to bring her husband. She told him that she had no husband. I knew that was true, but only if you left out a lot of information. He just told her that what she had said was true, she had been married to five husbands and was now living in the household of a man who was not her husband. He didn't say it in a mean or judging way. He never even asked about children. Perhaps he didn't want to add to her shame. "You must be a prophet," she told him. "But your people worship at Jerusalem, while my people worship on this mountain." As if to say that he could not be a prophet for her and her people.

"The day is coming," this prophet told her, "when the people of God will not worship on either mountain. God will employ the Jewish people to reach out to all the world. In fact that is happening even as we speak. You have to remember that God is Spirit and those who worship God must worship in Spirit and truth."

"I know that the Chosen One of God is coming. When the Chosen One of God comes to us, everything will be clear to us." The woman spoke slowly as if she was thinking out every word.

"I am the one you have waited for." The man was almost whispering. I wondered why he was making such a secret of it. No one came to the well at this time of day. Just then, though, a group of men who knew the Jewish prophet came up. They looked startled and very displeased that their friend was talking to a woman, a Samaritan woman at that.

Do you remember I told you that this was a love story, but not a romance? Well, I saw the way she looked at the prophet, and she looked like a woman who felt loved for the first time in her life. She left her water jar right here next to me and ran away. I wondered if what she was feeling frightened her away. Then the prophet's friends approached and asked if he wanted something to eat.

"I have food that you don't know anything about," was all he said as he stared off in the direction the woman had run.

"Did somebody bring him food while we were gone?" his friends asked each other. They looked more confused than the woman had been at the prophet's remarks.

Before long the woman returned, followed by a crowd of people. She must have told everyone in her village about what he had said. That was a pretty big change for someone who came to the well at noon to avoid her neighbors before.

"She said you told her everything she ever did. She said you are a prophet sent from God. She said you are the one we have waited for," the people said.

Older Elementary 3   **Reproducible 12B**

Bible Story

All her neighbors talked at once. When the prophet finally could quieten them down and could begin to teach them, they were so interested they couldn't get enough. He stayed on in the village for several days, living with the people and teaching them.

It was the strangest thing I had seen in all my centuries of providing water. Here was a Jew, the Chosen One of God, who came to his enemies instead of his own people. He claimed to have water that wiped away all thirst and food that even his friends didn't know anything about.

Instead of having his friends to announce his coming, he chose a Samaritan woman to speak for him among her own people.

It seemed that he was trying to make it as hard as possible for people to believe him. His message was so different, and it was presented in such an unusual way to such unlikely people.

Could it be that God chooses the people we least expect to tell us a message we may not be ready to hear? Could it be that a well as old as I am could learn something new? It is a deep subject, and I will have to dwell on it.

"Those who drink of the water that I will give them will never be thirsty."

John 4:14a

Reproducible 12C

Permission granted to photocopy for local church use. © 1998 Abingdon Press.

Choose one or more activities to bring the Bible to life.

Thirst Quenchers

Ask: Have you ever been really, really thirsty? Do you remember how much it helped to get a drink of water?

Give each student an equal number of salty crackers—at least fifteen to twenty if possible. **Say: I will use the slide flute to signal when to begin. You are to eat as many crackers as you can without drinking anything. When you have eaten all you can and really want a drink, put your head down on the table.**

When everyone has his or her head down, **say: This is how it feels to be very thirsty. Jesus talked about physical thirst, the kind that water quenches. But what happens after a while?** *(We get thirsty again.)*

Give each student a drink of water.

Supplies:
salty crackers, water, cups

Zillies:
slide flute

Thirst Stoppers

Divide the class into two teams. Place two one-gallon jars of water on a table in the center of the room. Have the teams positioned an equal distance from their water. Tell the teams which jar belongs to which team. (If you have a large class, divide the students into three or four teams and have three or four jars of water.)

Give each student a straw. **Say: I will use the slide flute to signal when to begin. The first player from each team runs to the team's jar and uses the straw to suck as much water out of the jar as possible. I will use the slide flute again to signal when to stop. With the same signal, the next player from both teams immediately runs to jars, puts in his or her straw, and begins sucking. I will use the slide flute to signal when they should stop and the next players begin.**

Repeat the relay several times. Each time increase the amount of time the players are to suck water through their straws, perhaps beginning with five seconds and ending with a full minute.

When the first jar is nearly empty, stop the relay. **Ask: Are you full of water now? Jesus spoke of a life-giving water that we could drink and never be thirsty again. Living water moves us toward God.**

Supplies:
two one-gallon jars of water, straws

Zillies:
slide flute

Life Zone

Choose one or more activities to bring the Bible to life.

Supplies:
Reproducible 12C, scissors

Zillies:
slide flute

Bible Verse Smuggle

Photocopy and cut out the Bible verse card **(bottom half, Reproducible 12C).** Ask the students to stand in a circle. Walk around the circle and select one person to be "It." Ask "It" to stand in the middle of the circle.

Say: "It" is going to stand in the middle of the circle. I will give someone in the circle the Bible verse card. Pass the card behind your backs around the circle. Be careful. If "It" can guess who is holding the card when I use the slide flute, the person holding the card has to try to say today's Bible verse. Then he or she becomes "It."

Read the verse to everyone. Use the slide flute to signal when to begin and stop. If the student holding the card is guessed and cannot say the verse, ask him or her to read the verse. Continue until several students have said the verse.

Supplies:
Reproducible 12E, cassette player

Zillies:
Cassette

Sing

Give each student a copy of the words to the song "Jesus in the Morning" **(Reproducible 12E).** Play the song on the **Cassette** and ask the students to follow along. Play the song again and invite everyone to sing.

Supplies:
small, clean bucket, small cups, water

Zillies:
none

Pray

Ask everyone to sit in a circle. Give each student a small cup. Walk inside the circle carrying a small, clean bucket of water.

Say: Jesus offers us life-giving water. As I come to you, dip your cup in the water and drink it. Each time, let's all pray: Lord, thank you for giving me living water, so that I may never be thirsty. Amen.

Give each student a copy of HomeZone to enjoy this week.

Home Zone For Students

Spray Wonders

Create a beautiful piece of art outdoors by using spray bottles. Collect empty spray bottles. Put water in each bottle. Add a little food coloring to each bottle and shake it well. Check to see if you have the color you want or if you need to add more food coloring.

Use clothespins to attach a large piece of paper to either a rope or a clothesline (outdoors, of course). Spray the paper using several colors of water. The colors will mix and create beautiful paintings. When you have finished your painting, take it down and lay it on the grass to dry.

You may want to wear a paint shirt or old clothes. Sometimes creating beauty can be messy work!

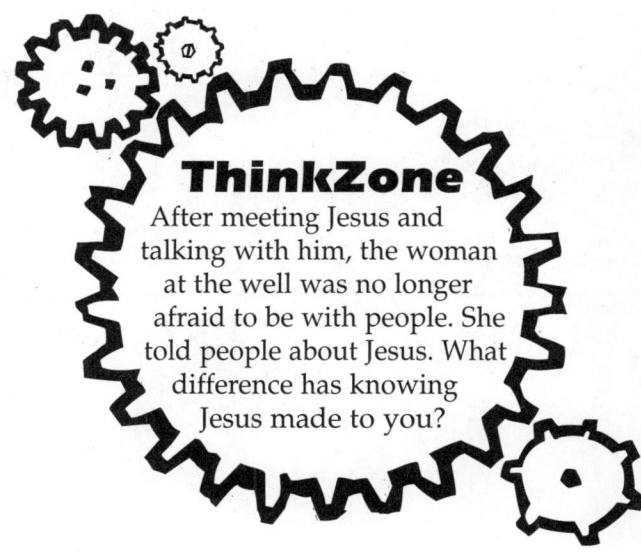

ThinkZone

After meeting Jesus and talking with him, the woman at the well was no longer afraid to be with people. She told people about Jesus. What difference has knowing Jesus made to you?

Memory Verse

"Those who drink of the water that I will give them will never be thirsty."
John 4:14a

Delicious Iced Tea Punch

Make a tasty drink for a large gathering of people—a special party or family time. Or make it to enjoy at mealtime or anytime. You will need:

3 large tea bags
3 quarts (which is 12 cups!) of boiling water
½ cup sugar
1 (12-ounce) can of frozen lemonade concentrate that has been thawed
1 (33-ounce) bottle of ginger ale that has been chilled in the refrigerator

Put the tea bags in the boiling water and let them boil for a minute or two. Turn the stove off and let them sit in the water for 8 minutes. Remove the tea bags. Pour the tea into a pitcher. Stir in the sugar and the lemonade concentrate. Chill in the refrigerator. Add the ginger ale when you are ready to serve the tea.

Jesus offers us living water.

Reproducible 12D

Permission granted to photocopy for local church use. © 1998 Abingdon Press.

BibleZone™

Song Zone

Jesus in the Morning

Jesus, Jesus
Jesus in the morning
Jesus in the noontime
Jesus, Jesus
Jesus when the sun goes down.

Love him, love him
Love him in the morning
Love him in the noontime
Love him, love him
Love him when the sun goes down.

Serve him, serve him
Serve him in the morning
Serve him in the noontime
Serve him, serve him
Serve him when the sun goes down
Down, down, down,
Why don't you—

Praise him, praise him
Praise him in the morning
Praise him in the noontime
Praise him, praise him
Praise him when the sun goes down
Down, down, down

Arr. © 1996 New Spring Publishing, Inc. (ASCAP), admin. by Brentwood-Benson Music Publishing, Inc. All rights reserved. Used by permission.

13 Bible

Jesus and Mary

Enter the Zone

Bible Verse
"This is my commandment, that you love one another as I have loved you."
John 15:12

Bible Story
John 11:17-20, 32-34, 38-44; 12:1-8

Mary of Bethany was the sister of Martha and Lazarus. We first heard of Mary when Jesus visited her home. Martha was frustrated that Mary was not helping but rather was merely sitting and listening to Jesus. Jesus gently rebuked Martha and assured her that Mary was doing the important thing. Mary was not simply practicing good hospitality, she was being attentive to her teacher whom she trusted completely.

According to John 12:1-8, Jesus visited their home again after he had raised Lazarus, the brother of Mary and Martha, from the dead. Later at dinner Martha was serving again while Lazarus and the others reclined at the table (a Greek custom). Mary entered the room carrying a jar of nard, an expensive perfume. She poured it on Jesus' feet and then wiped them with her hair. Judas Iscariot protested that the perfume could have been sold and the money could have been spent on the poor. But Jesus replied that the perfume was for his burial, and he added that he would not always be with them as the poor would be.

The ointment Mary used was a gesture of extravagant affection. The Song of Solomon mentions it as one of the perfumes giving fragrance to the king's couch (1:12) and one of several fragrant spices listed in praise of the bride (4:13-14). Being a rare perfume, its value could be compared to the wages a person would make in a year at that time.

Hospitality for travelers was customary. Often oils were used to soothe skin that had been parched in the hot sun. At the very least bread and water were offered, the traveler's feet were washed to remove the dust of travel, and the oil was applied to cool and refresh the body.

More than a custom of the day, hospitality was a demonstration of faithfulness to God.

We can show love to people in many ways.

Scope the Zone

ZONE	TIME	SUPPLIES	ZILLIES™
Zoom Into the Zone			
Get in the Zone	5 minutes	page 174, cassette player	Cassette
For Real?	10 minutes	Reproducible 13C, large jar, scissors	none
Sock It to Me	15 minutes	three pairs of extra large, long athletic socks; three pairs of large gloves; blindfolds	slide flute
BibleZone™			
Zoom Into the Bible	20 minutes	Bible for each student, Reproducible 13C, scissors, masking tape	sticky buddies, slide flute
A Loving Gesture	15 minutes	Reproducibles 13A and 13B	none
LifeZone			
Great Hall of Love	10 minutes	Reproducible 13D, markers, crayons	none
Echo-version	5 minutes	none	none
Gifts of Love	15 minutes	potpourri (or ingredients, see p. 162), scissors, glue, foil, tissue paper, glitter, empty butter tubs and lids	chipboard hearts
Sing 'n Praise	10 minutes	Reproducible 13E, cassette player, lotion	Cassette

Zillies™ are found in the **BibleZone™ FUNspirational™ Kit.**

OLDER ELEMENTARY 3

155

Zoom Into the Zone

Choose one or more activities to catch your children's interest.

Supplies:
page 174, cassette player

Zillies:
Cassette

Get in the Zone

Greet each student with a happy smile and say: **Welcome to the BibleZone!** Have "The Bible Zone" playing on the **Cassette**. Invite everyone to sing with you. Have copies of the words **(page 174)** available for anyone who needs them.

Supplies:
Reproducible 13C, large jar, scissors

Zillies:
none

For Real?

Cut apart the slips of customs **(top half, Reproducible 13C)** and put them in a jar. (The mouth of the jar should be wide enough that a child's hand can reach into the jar.)

Say: We will each take a turn reading a custom. Some of the customs may seem different to us. Let's decide if they are real or made up. After they are read, we will take a vote: Real? or Unreal?

After each slip is read and the vote is taken, tell the students whether the custom was real or unreal. (They are all real.) **Say: In Bible times there were many customs that may seem different to us. Today our Bible story will tell us about a custom that will really seem unusual to us.**

Supplies:
three pairs of extra large, long athletic socks; three pairs of large gloves; blindfolds

Zillies:
slide flute

Sock It to Me

Divide the students into three teams. Place three chairs in the front of the room. Have one player from each team sit in the chairs. Have everyone else sit on the floor facing them and be the cheering section.

Ask the three players sitting in the chairs to remove their shoes. Give each player a pair of extra large, long athletic socks and a pair of large gloves. Then blindfold each player.

Say: The contest is to see who can get both socks and both gloves on and then both socks and both gloves off first. I will use the slide flute to signal when to begin.

Continue play letting players from each team have turns. **Say: That was a crazy game! In Bible times, if you were a guest, someone would have actually helped you care for your hands and feet.**

BibleZone™

Bible

Choose one or more activities to immerse your children in the Bible story.

Zoom Into the Bible

Before class begins, try throwing a **sticky buddy** at the wall. They will adhere to most surfaces, but you may choose a door or side of a metal cabinet. Place a long strip of masking tape on the floor, six feet away from the surface you choose. Photocopy and cut out the questions **(bottom half, Reproducible 13C)** and have them ready to use.

Be certain each student has a Bible. Divide the students into three teams. Ask Team One to read John 11:17-20, 32-34. Ask Team Two to read John 11:38-44. Ask Team Three to read John 12:1-8. Ask the teams to tell what they read in the Bible, giving as much detail as possible.

Ask one player from each team to line up along the masking tape, facing the wall or whatever surface you have chosen. Give each player a sticky buddy.

Say: I will ask a question and use the slide flute. As soon as I use the slide flute, throw your sticky buddy at the wall. The first person who answers the question before the sticky buddy hits the floor wins that round. I will keep score to see which team wins the most rounds.

Have new players for each question. The sticky buddies can be rinsed and blotted dry with a paper towel if they become dirty.

Supplies:
Bible for each student, Reproducible 13C, masking tape, scissors

Zillies:
sticky buddies, slide flute

A Loving Gesture

Read or tell the story "A Family Friend" **(Reproducibles 13A and 13B)**. (For storytelling tips, read the article on pages 171 and 172.)

Encourage the students to talk with you about the following questions.
1. Why do you think Mary used the ointment on Jesus' feet?
2. Why do you think Mary wiped Jesus' feet with her hair?
3. What risk did Mary take when she put the ointment on Jesus' feet and wiped them with her hair?
4. What do you suppose the others who were there were thinking?
5. What do you suppose Jesus was thinking?
6. What is something you could do that would show as much affection for someone you love?

Supplies:
Reproducibles 13A and 13B

Zillies:
none

Bible Story

A Family Friend
by Michael Williams

Have you ever had such a good friend that you were willing to do anything for them? If they wanted it, you would give them your favorite book or baseball glove? You would play games you don't particularly care for just because they like to play them? When the big math test came up, you would let them use your lucky pencil? When the big game was to be played, you would let them borrow your lucky socks to wear (only if they promised not to let their parents wash them so that all the luck ran out)?

If you have ever had a friend like that, then you know something about how Mary felt about Jesus. Jesus was Mary's friend, her good friend. He had been a good friend to her whole family; her sister, Martha, and her brother, Lazarus. Jesus was such a good friend that he had done something no one else could have done for them. He had given them Lazarus back.

Mary's brother had gotten very, very sick. He was so sick that he could not get well, and finally he died. Mary and Martha had sent word for their friend, Jesus, to come because they thought Jesus might be able to heal their brother. But he didn't arrive in time. Lazarus died. Mary and Martha prepared Lazarus's body and it was placed into the tomb. It would stay there until all the flesh was gone, then his bones would be put into an ossuary, or bone box. Then that would be all that was left of the brother they loved.

Four days after Lazarus was placed in the tomb, Jesus arrived at the house of Mary and Martha. They were still crying and grieving for their brother. Mary was feeling so many emotions all at once. She was glad to see Jesus, but she was disappointed that he had not arrived in time to save Lazarus. She was upset that her friend, who could do so much for other people, could not help her brother.

Mary walked over to the place where Jesus sat and knelt at his feet. As she cried, her tears fell on his feet. Her first impulse was to wipe them off; but she had nothing to wipe them with, so she let the moment pass. Mary was so upset she said, "If you had only been here, Lazarus would not have died." She wasn't exactly blaming Jesus, she was just grieving and disappointed.

Later she thought she could have wiped her tears from Jesus' feet with her hair. Still, the teachers said that hair was a woman's glory and something that was very intimate, something that you didn't take down and let just anyone see.

Then Jesus got up. He prayed and called to Lazarus, "Come out." And much to everyone's amazement and Mary's delight, Lazarus got up and walked out in the very clothes they had dressed him in for burial. Jesus had given her back her brother. She had nothing valuable enough to give him in return. Not that Jesus seemed to want anything in return. He was just as happy as Mary and Martha were to have Lazarus back in the land of the living.

Still Mary thought about what she might do for Jesus to say thank you for the great gift he had given her. She thought and she thought. She thought until her head hurt.

Reproducible 13A

Permission granted to photocopy for local church use. © 1998 Abingdon Press.

Mary had very little of value, except those things that were needed around the house or for special occasions.

Many people from nearby Jerusalem had begun saying terrible things about Jesus. Some even said that he deserved to die for what he preached and the way he lived. When Mary heard these things, they broke her heart, and she realized the risk Jesus took every time he came to their house in Bethany, so near to Jerusalem. This just made her appreciate him more.

A short time after he had called Lazarus back from the grave, Jesus came to visit the family again. Mary was overwhelmed with feeling once more, but this time the feeling was gratitude. She was so grateful for his friendship. She was thankful that he, unlike most other men, listened to her and believed her thoughts were of value. And, of course, he had given her the gift of her brother's life.

Mary's mind searched throughout the house for a gift worthy of such a guest. The only thing she could think of was a bottle of spikenard, a perfume that usually would be saved for the burial of a member of the family. She ran and got out the expensive perfume. Almost before she realized what she was doing, Mary found herself kneeling at Jesus' feet a second time. This time it was not her tears that wet his feet. It was the perfume of the spikenard plant. The aroma was strong and quickly filled the whole house.

Mary realized that by now everyone in the room knew what she was doing, but she didn't care what they thought. Her only thought was to honor the friendship Jesus had shown her. So this time she took her hair down until it fell to its full length.

Then she wiped the perfume off Jesus' feet with her hair. She knew some people would be shocked by what she was doing. They would think it was too intimate and would scold her later. To show how she felt about Jesus was worth any scolding she might receive.

The scolding didn't take long in coming. One of Jesus' followers, Judas Iscariot, spoke up, "Such expensive perfume should have been sold and used to help the poor." He kept the money for Jesus' group, but had not seemed too concerned about the poor in the past.

Jesus said, "Leave her alone. She was saving this perfume for the time I will be dead and buried. Judas, I am pleased to see that you have developed such a concern for the poor. You will always have them with you, and I expect you to take care of them. You do not realize it now, but you will not always have me with you."

Judas stalked out of the room, but Jesus stayed and talked with Mary and the others. They ate and they laughed the rest of the day. It was hard to imagine a time when Jesus would not be with them.

Long after Jesus left the house, the aroma of spikenard lingered. Every time Mary smelled it, she thought of her friend Jesus. Little did she know that Jesus was about to do something that would call forth her everlasting gratitude. And ours.

Custom #1: In Greece on New Year's Day, children eat cake that has a hidden coin in it.	**Custom #7:** In Bangladesh, men eat supper first; then the women and children share what is left.
Custom #2: In Iran, New Year's Day is celebrated in March.	**Custom #8:** In Japan, people wash with soap and water, rinse off, and then get in a tub of water to soak. No soap is used in the tub.
Custom #3: In Ghana, a child is given several names, including one that tells the time of day, day of the week, or the special event that was taking place when the child was born.	**Custom #9:** In China, when a child loses a baby tooth, it is buried in the ground if it is an upper tooth. It is tossed onto rooftops if it is a lower tooth.
Custom #4: In Germany, some children sleep on feather mattresses that are so soft that they literally sink into them.	**Custom #10** In Nigeria and Tanzania, two countries in Africa, there is no school during the rainiest time of the year.
Custom #5: In Indonesia, touching someone on the head is considered bad luck.	**Custom #11:** In Russia, children will have a birthday pie more often than a birthday cake.
Custom #6: In Italy, children trace an invisible cross on their chest as a sign that they will keep a promise.	**Custom #12:** In Spain on New Year's Eve, people eat a dozen grapes while the clocks chime twelve.

1. Who was Lazarus?

2. What happened to Lazarus before Jesus arrived?

3. How did Mary react when Jesus arrived?

4. What did Jesus do for Lazarus?

5. What did Mary do to show her love for Jesus?

6. What did Judas Iscariot say about Mary's gift to Jesus?

Choose one or more activities to bring the Bible to life.

Great Hall of Love

Give each student a copy of the illustration of Mary wiping Jesus' feet with her hair **(Reproducible 13D)**. Say: It took great love for Mary to do this. A woman did not let her hair be shown except privately at home. Also Mary used an ointment that cost as much money as many people made in a year in Bible times. Her love for Jesus was so great that she gave the most wonderful gift she had.

Invite the students to color the pictures using their finest art skills. Plan where to display the illustration, perhaps in the hallway of your church or near the narthex.

Supplies:
Reproducible 13D, crayons, markers

Zillies:
none

Echo-version

Say: I will say John 15:12, our Bible verse for today. After I say a part of the Bible verse, I will point at you and you will repeat the last two words. When we have said the entire verse, say the complete verse with me two times. Lead the students as follows:

Leader: *This is*
Students: *This is*
Leader: *This is my*
Students: *is my*
Leader: *This is my commandment,*
Students: *my commandment,*
Leader: *This is my commandment, that*
Students: *commandment, that*
Leader: *This is my commandment, that you*
Students: *that you*
Leader: *This is my commandment, that you love*
Students: *you love*
Leader: *This is my commandment, that you love one*
Students: *love one*
Leader: *This is my commandment, that you love one another*
Students: *one another*
Leader: *This is my commandment, that you love one another as*
Students: *another as*
Leader: *This is my commandment, that you love one another as I*
Students: *as I*
Leader: *This is my commandment, that you love one another as I have*
Students: *I have*

Supplies:
none

Zillies:
none

OLDER ELEMENTARY 3

Life Zone

Choose one or more activities to bring the Bible to life.

Leader: *This is my commandment, that you love one another as I have loved*
Students: *have loved*
Leader: *This is my commandment, that you love one another as I have loved you.*
Students: *loved you.*
All: *This is my commandment, that you love one another as I have loved you.*
All: *This is my commandment, that you love one another as I have loved you.*

Gifts of Love

Supplies:
potpourri or ingredients (see p. 162), scissors, glue, foil, tissue paper, glitter, empty butter tubs and lids

Zillies:
chipboard hearts

Give each student a **chipboard heart.** Offer a variety of ways to decorate the heart: using foil, glitter and glue, or tissue paper and glue. When the hearts are decorated, set them aside.

Give each student a small empty butter tub and lid. Glue the chipboard hearts onto the lids and let them dry. Plan to have enough potpourri to fill the tubs. (Or let the students make their own using six whole nutmegs, five cinnamon sticks, three vanilla beans, ½ cup whole cloves, one tablespoon crushed anise seed, one tablespoon ground allspice, and ½ cup ground orris root.)

Say: We can give these potpourri gifts to our friends to express our feelings.

Sing 'n Praise

Supplies:
Reproducible 13E, cassette player, lotion

Zillies:
Cassette

Give each student a copy of the words to the song "Is There Anything I Can Do for You?" **(Reproducible 13E).** Play the song on the **Cassette** and ask the students to follow along. Play the song again and invite everyone to sing with you.

If you think your students will be comfortable with the experience, let them put lotion on one another's feet or hands while the music plays.

Pray: Dear Lord, we thank you for your great love. You have shown us how to love one another. You have shown us to give love to all people. Be with us each day and help us to live the love you have shown us. Amen.

Give each student a copy of HomeZone to enjoy this week.

Home Zone For Students

My, what a LOVE-ly cake!

You can make a cake that your family will love. First you will need to make homemade whipped cream.

You will need:
1 pint of whipping cream
3 tablespoons confectioner's sugar
1 teaspoon vanilla extract
Put the tongs of the beater and a metal mixing bowl in your freezer for 20 minutes. Pour all of the ingredients in the bowl and mix on high speed until soft peaks form. Store the whipped cream in the refrigerator until you are ready to use it.

Now make your cake. You will need:
24 graham crackers
½ cup chocolate syrup
your homemade whipped cream
miniature chocolate chips

First whip the chocolate syrup into the whipped cream. Arrange 4 graham crackers on a plate. Spread chocolate whipped cream on the layers. Put 4 graham crackers on top of the chocolate whipped cream. Spread chocolate whipped cream on the graham crackers. Repeat the layers until you have used all the graham crackers. Put chocolate whipped cream on the top and sides of the cake. Sprinkle miniature chocolate chips over the top of the cake. Keep the cake in the refrigerator until you are ready to serve it.

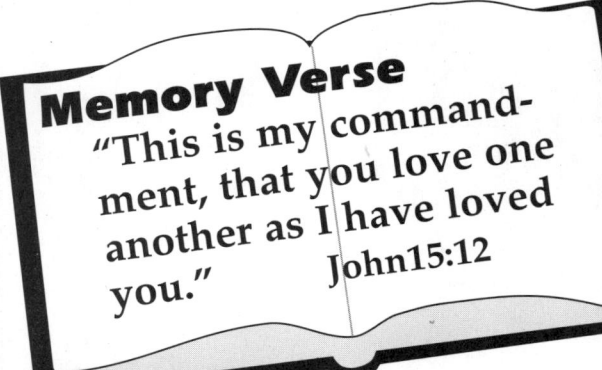

Memory Verse
"This is my commandment, that you love one another as I have loved you." John 15:12

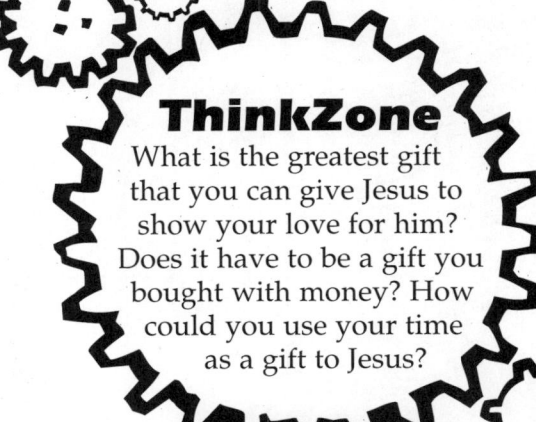

ThinkZone
What is the greatest gift that you can give Jesus to show your love for him? Does it have to be a gift you bought with money? How could you use your time as a gift to Jesus?

We can show love to people in many ways.

Song Zone

Is There Anything I Can Do for You?

Is there anything I can do for you?
Is there anything I can do?
For all the things you've done for me,
Is there anything I can do?
I'm willing to be used, dear Lord,
What e'er the price may be.
So if there's anything I can do for you,
just make it known to me.

Is there anywhere I can go for you?
Is there anywhere I can go?
For the places you have been for me,
Is there anywhere I can go?
I'm willing to be used, dear Lord,
Whate'er the price may be.
So if there's anywhere I can go for you,
just make it known to me.
Just make it known to me.

© 1977 by John T. Benson Publishing (ASCAP)/Bridge Building Music, Inc. (BMI), admin. by Brentwood-Benson Music Publishing, Inc. All rights reserved. Used by permission.

Reproducible 13E
Permission granted to photocopy for local church use. © 1998 Abingdon Press.

Game Zone

Bible Verse Golf

Learning Bible verses does not have to be boring or difficult if you approach the activity as a game. Older elementary boys and girls enjoy friendly competition.

For Bible verse golf you will need these items: sheets of colored construction paper (one piece for each word of the Bible verse), masking tape, recycled newspaper sheets, ping-pong balls, and a large carpeted open area.

Roll each piece of construction paper into a tube. Secure with tape. Write one word of the Bible verse on each tube. Arrange the tubes at random around the room. Secure the tubes to the floor with loops of masking tape.

Let each student create a golf club from tightly rolled sheets of newspaper. Secure the edges with masking tape.

Boys and girls will play a "round" of golf by hitting the ping-pong balls through the word tubes in order of the Bible verse. Play several rounds and post the best scores.

Goop Diving

Nothing inspires group participation like a little mess and this activity makes a lot of mess.

For Goop Diving you will need: a small child-sized swimming pool full of Goop, plastic coins or other objects, recycled newspaper, and a plastic drop cloth.

Goop: 6 boxes of cornstarch (16 ounce boxes), 15 cups of water, food coloring. Empty the boxes of cornstarch into the plastic swimming pool. Add water and food coloring. Mix. (You can make Goop in smaller quantities for individual gooping. Use one box of cornstarch, 2 ½ cups of water for a smaller batch.)

Cover the area with newspaper. Then place the plastic drop cloth on top of the newspaper. Center the plastic swimming pool on the drop cloth. Drop the coins (or other objects) into the swimming pool. Mix until the coins sink to the bottom. Have the children get down on their knees around the swimming pool. The object of the game is to retrieve as many coins (or other objects) as possible in two minutes. The fun is the harmless goopy mess. One minute the goop is solid, the next it is a soupy liquid. Stand back and enjoy.

Game Zone

What a Team!

Every lesson suggests that the students be divided into teams. You can use a variety of methods to create teams. That way the students are not bored and they are not always on the same team!

Try some of these suggestions:
1. Divide by birthdays. The first six students born in the calendar year are on one team, the next six are on another team.

2. Put all the students' names in a paper bag. Draw out two names. Those students become the Team Leaders. Let them take turns drawing names until everyone is on a team.

3. Have the students line up in order by height. Select every other student to be on the same team.

4. Have the students line up in alphabetical order of their first names. Divide the line in half.

Badminton Bible Verses

Your serve! Learn the Bible verse and play a game of indoor badminton at the same time.

You will need: a wire coat hanger for each child, hose, wire twist ties, sponge balls.

Pull the wire coat hangers into an elongated diamond shape. Bend the hook of the coat hanger into the neck so there is no sharp edge exposed. Stretch one of the hose over each wire frame. Leave about three inches at the top. Gather together with a wire twist tie. Wrap the remainder of the hose around the handle to pad it and protect the hand from the hook.

Divide the boys and girls into groups of two. Each player should have a racquet and a ball. The first player hits the sponge ball and says the first word of the Bible verse. The second player returns the sponge ball to the first player saying the second word of the Bible verse. This continues until the Bible verse is completed. If a player forgets the next word or misses the ball, the opposing player gets the point. A wild shot that is impossible to return is a point for the opposing player. Play until one player gets to twenty-one or for however long you feel is appropriate for your class.

Art Zone

Ready, Set, Create!

Older elementary boys and girls enjoy expressing themselves creatively. But they may get bored with activities they consider to be "the same old thing." They enjoy large projects and can work well individually or as a group. They want to be recognized for individual talents and efforts, but they also take pride in peer group identity and accomplishments.

Older elementary boys and girls also enjoy making things for other people. Included here are several projects that would work well as projects for others. They may, however, take more than the allotted time and require materials that are a little more difficult to get. But they are unique and will produce excellent results. If you have time for special projects and discover that your students love art adventures, try some of these projects.

Bubble Art

Supplies: plastic drinking straws, tempera paint (various colors), paper, dish washing soap, plastic spoons, old cookie sheet, small bowl, cup of water

1. Place 10 spoonfuls of tempera paint, 1 spoonful of dish washing soap, and 1 spoonful of water in the small bowl. Stir until mixed. Put a straw in and blow gently.
2. When the bubbles rise about an inch above the edge of the bowl, curl a piece of paper and gently touch it to the bubbles. Do not let the paper touch the rim of the bowl.
3. Lift the paper and see the bubble painting. Let it dry, then add another color.

BubbleArt makes wonderful gift wrap as well as creative designs for the fronts of cards and Bible verse posters.

Art Zone

Puffy Top Gifts Boxes

Supplies: mixing bowl, food coloring, spoon, glue and acrylic varnish, flour, salt, water, scissors, small cardboard gift boxes, construction paper, pencil, plastic squeeze bottles (The kind that mustard and ketchup are often served in are perfect.)

1. Turn the top of the box to be covered upside down on the paper. Draw around the edges. Cut out the paper and glue it to the top of the box.
2. Draw a simple design on the top of the box with a pencil.
3. Fill in the design with puffy paint. Let it dry overnight.
4. Brush on a coat of acrylic varnish to protect the work and make it shiny. Let that dry.
5. Fill the box with special treasures, notes, or anything you think that person will enjoy.

Puffy Paint

Mix one cup flour, 1 cup water, and 1 cup salt together. Divide evenly into several small dishes. Add food coloring to each dish to make a different color. Experiment to create new and different colors.

If you have more than one squeeze bottle, fill each one with a different color. If you have only one bottle, squeeze one color in all the places you want that color to be. Then wash the bottle and use it for the other colors, one at a time.

Make the Bible the Book They Love

Welcome to BibleZone™! These lessons are written especially to help the Bible become the book your students love the most. There are many things you can do to open the Bible to children. Many of the lessons have simple suggestions of things to do that will help your students build Bible skills. We want the message of the Bible to speak to children so they can live in response to the good news they find in the Scriptures.

Each week there is a memory verse for the students to learn. Memorizing Bible verses is an important skill for older elementary children to acquire. However, memorization can become a threat to their self-esteem unless cooperative memorization techniques are used. Instead of asking for individuals to recite in front of others, use a team approach in which the students help one another. Reinforce memorization in fun ways—in a song, through art projects, by playing games, or acting out the verses. Help them learn long passages by breaking them into shorter phrases and assigning phrases to teams. Have teams say their phrases in order to repeat the verses. If you have written phrases on index cards, swap the cards around for the teams to learn new phrases. Continue swapping the cards until everyone has learned the verse.

BibleZone™ is fun! But in the midst of the fun there will be some serious learning happening! Make your own personal goals as you teach to help your students

- recognize the Bible as a revelation of God and a record of how people have experienced God;
- and explore the meaning of Bible stories;
- learn the names of all the books of the Bible;
- learn how the Bible came to be;
- know that there are many translations and versions of the Bible;
- recognize sections of the Bible: Law, History, Poetry and Songs, Prophets, Gospels, Letters;
- learn to use tools such as a concordance, an atlas, and a Bible dictionary;
- explore stories in historical context;
- recognize the important role the Bible has had throughout history;
- recognize the Bible as the source of some worship resources used in their church;
- know that the Bible was written by many people over a long period of time;
- grow in their understanding of the relationship between the Bible message and their own relationship with God.

Enter the Story Zone
by Dr. Michael Williams

So you think you're not a storyteller. When was the last time someone asked you about a recent trip? What did you tell them? A story, most likely. Or what did you say when you saw that friend you had not seen for years? Didn't you swap stories of the years since you last met?

Most of us tell some stories each day, even if it is just to let a spouse or friend know how our day has gone. Storytelling comes so naturally to us that most of us don't realize that we are practicing the same art that brought us the stories of the Bible.

Why Tell Stories?

As teachers of children, you tell Bible stories as naturally as talking to your closest friend. The goal of telling Bible stories is to show, through the ancient narratives of faith, God's presence in the students' lives today. Keep in mind that storytelling in the classroom is not performance or entertainment; biblical storytelling is acquainting listeners with biblical family and deepening the loving relationship you have already begun with your students. Most important, you are deepening each student's relationship with God.

When you tell Bible stories to your students, you
• let them know that they belong to the family of faith;
• provide companions for their spiritual journey;
• provide them with the basic content of faith through examples of God's creative presence with our ancestors;
• and let them see God's creative presence in their own lives.

As the storyteller, you are serving as tour guide through the ancient world of the Bible. Although many of you may feel more comfortable in the role of teacher than in the role of storyteller, you each bring all the necessary tools; all you need is a body, a voice, and an imagination! Without your guidance and knowledge your students will miss the incredible sights, sounds, smells, and experiences. Be sure each story you tell invites their senses. And don't worry! Much of the information you will need can be found in the lesson material, but sometimes it will be helpful look at a Bible dictionary, commentary, or other biblical reference book to help identify characters, objects, and customs of particular interest.

Using Your Imagination

Your imagination as a storyteller can spark the imaginations of your students. The information you gather from the lesson, a Bible dictionary, or a laymen's guide can help create the world of the story. Don't be afraid to embellish the story with details that "might have been." Give students enough information to imagine for themselves. Imagination simply involves offering enough detail for your listener to actively participate in creating the story world. The artistry is in giving enough detail without overdoing it, and without getting bogged down in too many details. You want to allow your students enough imaginative room to do their part in creating the story.

What About Gestures?

How comfortable are you with your body? Your use of movement in storytelling will depend on your comfort with your body and its range of movement. A simple gesture can show an emotion or

the size of an object or the height of a character. It is always appropriate to sing a Bible story song or involve the students in acting out the story after you have told it.

Emphasize With Your Voice

Your voice is the most effective tool you have to communicate the energy and feelings for an effectively told story. If a character you are describing is happy, sad, afraid, or ashamed, your voice must communicate that. If the tone of a story is somber or suspenseful or fanciful, show it by the tone of your voice. If you are having a difficult time holding the attention of your listeners, use a trick that storytellers have employed for centuries: instead of raising your voice, speak more softly. This will draw your listeners into the story, sometimes encouraging them to literally lean in to hear more clearly.

Older Elementary Children

Older elementary children like stories! In fact, the characters and stories often seem more interesting to older elementary children when the teacher reads or tells stories aloud. The role of storytelling expands as the students get to know the members of their biblical family. The characters in these Bible stories become their familiar companions and will then accompany them through life, reminding them of their faith and of the values of those who follow the Scriptures and Jesus' teachings. When we tell stories to this age group we are both populating and strengthening their inner world.

Bible people made real through storytelling accompany children, teens, and adults through life. When children must move out of familiar surroundings, say to a strange house and neighborhood, Abraham and Sarah will go with them. When they face their worst fears, young David will stand beside them with his sling and five smooth stones. When they are the new kid in class, feeling very much like a foreigner, Ruth the Moabite will speak words of hope and courage. When they go off into the "far country" of disobedience and alienation, Jesus' prodigal son will whisper words of forgiveness and home and they will look for the welcoming father figure.

Older elementary children can deal with more of the content of faith than younger children. This may include the historical or cultural background that can be found either in the lesson or any good Bible dictionary or a resource like *The Storyteller's Companion to the Bible* (Abingdon). To complement the story, encourage the students to put the story into action by constructing scale model buildings of the period, making costumes, and acting out the story.

We know that stories shape decision making. We Christians are a people with a specific set of stories that we claim are sacred to us. Those stories are contained in the Bible. The choices we make are a reflection of the stories we live. So our ethics take shape as we learn the stories of our faith tradition. Stories that are not from the Bible, but are drawn from the history of the people of faith, can also be helpful as we are formed in the peculiar people God has called us to become.

Perhaps the most important thing to remember in telling Bible stories to persons of any age is that, as Christians, the story we have to tell is a love story. We are like children on the playground passing along a love note to a beloved child that reads "Did you know God loves you?" This is our calling: To tell stories about the God who loves all of us to people we have come to love. This is also one of the greatest privileges anyone can have.

Adapted from "Telling Bible Stories," by Michael Williams, *Children's Teacher*, Summer 1997.

Bible ONE™	Bible ONE™
Bible ONE™	Bible ONE™
Bible ONE™	Bible ONE™
Bible ONE™	Bible ONE™

Permission granted to photocopy for local church use. © 1998 Abingdon Press.

The Bible Zone

Where else can we find a lesson learned on every page?
Stories that have lived to teach us all from age to age.
From the flood to parting waters, burning bushes,
   prophets, scholars,
God's Word takes us anywhere.

In the Bible Zone where God's Word come to life.
In the Bible Zone our path is always bright.
A book for all creation to every boy and girl.
In the Bible Zone is God's treasure for the world.

Learning of forgiveness or when learning how to pray,
God's word gives examples of the things we face each day
When we choose to look inside we see ahead or back in time.
God's word takes us anywhere.

In the Bible Zone where God's Word come to life.
In the Bible Zone our path is always bright.
A book for all creation to every boy and girl.
In the Bible Zone is God's treasure for the world.

In the Bible Zone where God's Word come to life.
In the Bible Zone our path is always bright.
A book for all creation to every boy and girl.
In the Bible Zone is God's treasure for the world.

Words: David Hampton
© 1997 New Spring Publishing, Inc. (ASCAP), admin. by Brentwood-Benson Music, Inc.
All Rights Reserved. Used by permission.

Comments From Users

Use the following scale to rate BibleZone™ resources
If you did not use a section, write "Did not use" in the Comments space.

1 = In No Lessons   2 = In Some Lessons   3 = In Most Lessons   4 = In All Lessons

1. *Enter the Zone* provided information that helped me teach this lesson's Scripture.
   1   2   3   4   Comments:

2. The *Scope the Zone* chart made lesson planning easy.
   1   2   3   4   Comments:

3. The teaching plan was organized in a way that made it easy to use.
   1   2   3   4   Comments:

4. The Teacher's Guide provided easy-to-follow instructions for the learning activities.
   1   2   3   4   Comments:

5. The supplies necessary to do the activities were easily located in my home or church.
   1   2   3   4   Comments:

6. My students were able to understand the lesson's ZoneIn™.
   1   2   3   4   Comments:

7. The activities matched the learning level and abilities of my students.
   1   2   3   4   Comments:

8. The number of activities in the lesson plan worked for the time I had available (indicate how much time):_____.
   If not, check:_____ too many _____ too few.
   1   2   3   4   Comments:

9. I used activities from the "GameZone" section of the Teacher's Guide.
   1   2   3   4   Comments:

10. I used activities from the "ArtZone" section of the Teacher's Guide.
    1   2   3   4   Comments:

11. I used information from articles I read in the Teacher's Guide.
    1   2   3   4   Comments:

12. I used the Cassette in my classroom.
    1   2   3   4   Comments:

13. I used items from the BibleZone™ FUNspirational™ Kit
    1   2   3   4   Comments:

14. I sent the HomeZone™ page home to students.
    1   2   3   4   Comments:

Older Elementary 3

Permission granted to photocopy for local church use. © 1998 Abingdon Press.

ADDITIONAL COMMENTS

Activities my students enjoy the most are:

Activities my students enjoy the least are:

I use BibleZone™ for_____Sunday School _____Second Hour Sunday School _____Children's Church _____Wednesday nights _____Sunday nights _____Children's Fellowship _____other

ABOUT MY CLASS

Number of Students at Each Age in My Class:

_____Age 9 _____Age 10 _____Age 11 _____Age 12

_____Other (Specify)_____

Average number of students who attend my class each week:_____

I teach: _____alone _____with another teacher each week

_____taking turns with other teachers _____with an adult helper

ABOUT MY CHURCH

_____Rural _____Small Town _____Downtown _____Suburban

_____Under 200 Members _____200-700 Members _____Over 700 Members

Church Name and Address: _____

_____

My Name and Address: _____

_____

Please return this form to   Susan Salley
Research Department
201 8th Ave., So
P.O. Box 801
Nashville, TN 37202-0801